PERILS
OF
TRANQUILITY

PERILS OF TRANQUILITY

BOITSHOKO JEREMIA

authorHOUSE®

AuthorHouse™
1663 Liberty Drive
Bloomington, IN 47403
www.authorhouse.com
Phone: 1-800-839-8640

© *2013 by Boitshoko Jeremia. All rights reserved.*

No part of this book may be reproduced, stored in a retrieval system, or transmitted by any means without the written permission of the author.

Published by AuthorHouse   03/12/2013

ISBN: 978-1-4817-2930-7 (sc)
ISBN: 978-1-4817-2931-4 (e)

Library of Congress Control Number: 2013904733

Any people depicted in stock imagery provided by Thinkstock are models, and such images are being used for illustrative purposes only.
Certain stock imagery © *Thinkstock.*

This book is printed on acid-free paper.

Because of the dynamic nature of the Internet, any web addresses or links contained in this book may have changed since publication and may no longer be valid. The views expressed in this work are solely those of the author and do not necessarily reflect the views of the publisher, and the publisher hereby disclaims any responsibility for them.

Contents

Introduction vii
Plowing Among Cape Buffalos 1
The Snake And The Toilet 6
The Lion Bidder 8
Mum And The Elephant 12
The Lions Of Pandamatenga 22
Border Python 28
Game Wardens 31
Xaxaba 33
A Night In The Forest 36
The Wrath Of The Zambezi Rapids 40
George And The Hyena 51
Sleep My Dog 54
Running Naked 57
A Kill In Front Of My House 60
The Water Buck 63
The Price Of Adultery 68
A Day At The Grazing Pastures 71
Waiting For Death 74
A Moment Away 77
The Making Of Ultimate Rangers 83
Ten O'clock Is My Time 90
Gathering Fire Wood 93
Please Help Me 95
The Pregnant Teenager 97
Die Hard Warthogs 99
Matavanero 101

Introduction

On January 1st, 2011, I went as a tourist to Victoria Falls, Zimbabwe using a bus from a tour company. There was a lady that was in the bus with me who had taken her aunt from Mauritius to go see the falls. Over lunch hour at a restaurant that I cannot remember, she asked me how we locals from our country lived in an area that has wildlife animals. She was really interested in hearing the stories, something a standard tourist who spends the night in a hotel does not know. So I, and Michael my friend, our tour guide, began telling her what she wanted to know. By the time our meals were served we had said enough for her to say 'You guys should write a book. Do you know how much people will want to hear this! If you don't do it somebody will come and write it.' I did not believe a word of what she said at the time. She invited me to share what I had told her with members of Francistown Rotary club. I brought up all the excuses I could think of. After six months I honored her request though I did not see any use in any of it. But a seed had been sown in the soils of my heart six months before at that restaurant in Victoria Falls. She kept watering the seed. It was in Francistown where my eyes were fully open to what she had been talking to me about. After my presentation, I saw that indeed I had to write down these experiences in story format of our side of the story as people who live in areas of tourism and wildlife. This book is a result of that conversation we had during that January 1st lunch hour in a foreign land, both of us being strangers to each other.

I now share with you, another stranger, more than what I shared with a person who was a stranger at the time. I collected stories from a number of people, never the less, most of them are my own experiences, like the last two in the book and the first few chapters herein. I did use different names to keep consistency with the names of people that had given me their stories, such as that of my good friend Morgan Ncube. I did alter names of almost all the people in the book to hide their identity for security reasons.

This book would not have been written if it was not for the advice and interest of that lady who was a stranger back then, though it comes to you after two years. That lady is none other than Saadia Rosenkhan. I am indebted to you my friend.

I hope the reader will enjoy the stories. I strived to make the sad ones to be not so sad. I did try to make some of them hilarious. Africa is still the best place to be. Let not the stories paint a picture in your mind to feel sorrowful or lack interest in visiting the countries mentioned here. Most of them are from Botswana. It is my pleasure sharing them with you. Enjoy them.

1
PLOWING AMONG CAPE BUFFALOS

My father owned a tractor that we used to make extra income from during the rainy season by plowing for interested farmers in Kavimba village. Often after exhausting the Kavimba market, he would move to the last village in the Chobe enclave area, Mbalakalungu. As a boy in my mid-teens he liked engaging me in this farming business.

He did not actually use the tractor himself; he hired a driver who was also a qualified mechanic. In a day we would plow about six hectors, the tractor was small. The plow was small too. So six hectors impressed us, we thought that it was a lot; we knew otherwise after we met tractors that are used in commercial farms.

One December morning, while it was raining we decided to go and plow for Mr. Johnson about five kilometers out of our village in the plains near the Botswana-Namibia border line. He wanted us to plow only two hectors of his field. I think it was after 8am. Four people went out for the task that he wanted us to do. Our tractor worker, Goliath, Heita, Johnson and I got on the Messy Ferguson 135 tractor. The field owner had a riffle for birds. He asked me to carry it for him, otherwise he couldn't seat very well on the tractor. He gave me the gun and not the bullets. Heita got hold of the seeds; a 12.5kg maize bag from the government.

Upon arriving at his field, I noticed some white egrets on the reeds. I asked the meaning of the egrets in the wilderness so far from cattle that were in our village. The reply I got is that the egrets had spent a night in that place. I was not satisfied with the answer. Birds are usually up early. They rarely rise up at 8am, in fact it is impossible for a wild bird to rise up at that time. The second thing that raised my doubts is the fact that egrets are associated with cattle. Although I had not seen their nests, if they have any nests, I still could not believe that they could sleep that far in the wilderness.

In my amazement, the reed tops started to move. I directed their attention towards the moving reeds top. My curiosity was dismissed as cowardice. It is only a breeze, do not mind it. We got off the tractor. The old man, Johnson, led the way, showing us where he had plowed the previous year. He had to show us the boundaries of his field and where he plowed the previous year because the water reeds grow so fast every year and it needed somebody that was familiar with the place to guide the new comers.

By the way, in Kavimba, that lies 78km west of Kasane, plowing is done on the flood plains. When the Chobe River gets flooded every year in February, all the fields get submerged in water and there is nothing that farmers reap out of it. Some people have given up arable farming, but not our client. For us it was more of making money and not the floods, we had nothing to lose. The farmer lost it both ways, we gained, it was purely business.

After the arrival of the floods, the water reeds grew very fast. They grew so tall that even wild animals, including the stately elephants, could not be seen once they were in the reeds. I do not know how many meters in height they grew. Wild animals loved hiding in the reeds during the day, especially if they delayed to go back to the forest when they descended to the river and the plains in search of water. Those that did not make it back before sunrise remained in the reeds all day until sunset that is when they would go back into the forest.

Johnson led the way down the little plateau that was in his field that did not have any reeds. We marched in a single line. The old man in front, followed after a meter by Goliath, then I followed in third place, and finally Heita was at the back. He was not carrying the sack of seeds; I had the gun with me. I was moving with it without any bullets.

We did a lot of chatting as we walked. We made a turn to the west, which was on our right. 'This is where I plowed last year, all of this place I did it,' that was Johnson. 'The soil will be easier to till because we once plowed it.' Then at timed intervals he would shout 'hey' in the midst of his sentences like somebody who is chasing away birds. 'We plowed this whole place . . . . hey . . .' In between his sentence the tall reeds opened up like a scroll. Death had paid us an unexpected visit and there was none of us who were prepared to meet face to face with it. Personally I thought we had woken up an elephant from its sleep. We all ran for our lives. There were no trees around; mind you we were in the plains. The tallest thing was the reeds that were a habitation to these dangerous animals. Running five kilometers to safety did not look like an option for me. I had so much faith that I would make it to Kavimba alive. The old man who was limping before out ran all of us, I was position three. Goliath was between me and Johnson. I threw the gun away in the process; it had become a useless burden with no bullets. Goliath lost his hat. I stepped on Heita's slippers and damaged them. He kept shouting at me, 'my shoes, you have destroyed my shoes.' We were in a life and death situation and all that this boy thought about was his slipper shoes. I ignored him.

Reaching clear ground, Goliath rushed towards the tractor. I turned from running to Kavimba to him, I changed course. We had another problem. The ignition system of our tractor wasn't working; we brought the engine to live mechanically by placing two terminals together. Goliath hit the two terminals together and the tractor roared to life. He revved the engine repeatedly for some time. Then at a distance of about two kilometers we saw a large heard of buffaloes coming out of the reeds towards the north. I had been right all along, even though I had been labeled as a coward earlier. Which meant that what we had run away from were actually male buffaloes that keep guard to the larger heard. Guard buffaloes never move in large numbers, it's either a single buffalo or they would form a group of six.

We got on the tractor and went back in search of the gun and the hat that had fallen. It's only now that I realize the kind of risk we were taking in going back into the reeds with an open, small tractor. I mean, had these wild buffaloes decided to give us a course on basic animal behavior, I do not know what would have become of us on that tractor; four people on it. We managed to locate the gun and the hat.

'You are so stupid, how could you throw away the gun like that!' jabbed the old man. 'You are the one to blame old man. I long asked you to give me the bullets but you refused saying I will waste your bullets. This is the results of your refusal.' I defended myself.

We never went back to that field again, it has been over ten years now and I have never went back there again. Life is too precious to be wasted in the early hours of the morning. At least I learnt that some old people can out run youth and middle aged men. We had undermined Christopher's ability to run faster than any of us. Thank God none of us lost their lives that morning, although some that were present that morning have passed away due to other causes.

2

THE SNAKE AND THE TOILET

One night my blind grandmother called for her grandchildren to come and help her with something. There was no answer. She called again and there was no answer. Everybody was at the main house watching television. She had remained alone in her house, like she often does. She is not a television person like people of this generation. She is also blind; she has nothing to do with watching television.

Every night after supper she would seat on the steps that lead into her house, and after sometime she would get inside. Whenever I am home I enjoy sitting with her and chat about a lot of things.

Somehow she decided to go the toilet. It is located at the corner of the compound, there is no light switch inside to be used during the night. One has to carry their own light to see when they went there at night. With her there was no need for the light.

She made her way through, finally reaching the toilet. Once inside she raised the toilet cover. She heard something hissing. She stood still, extended her hand towards the toilet seat again. Some more hissing came from the toilet. Then she let go of the toilet seat cover. Went back to the house and called for the grandchildren to go and see what was in the toilet. My mother, my aunt and some cousins rushed there. They lit a torch into the toilet and found a very long snake, over a meter in length with part of its body lying under the seat cover. It was intending to cross over the seat and climb the wall to go outside. Grandma pressed it with the seat cover and left it in that position until her children came over to see.

They tried killing it with a stick unfortunately there was not enough space in the toilet for such a task. My aunt's husband brought a gun to shoot it, but they decided to leave it alone hoping that it will free itself when they were gone. When they returned the following morning they found it in the same position that they had left it in the previous night. It did not move an inch. My cousins ended up killing it, for they needed the service of the toilet.

Speculations as to why the snake never moved an inch the whole night arose. The widely accepted one, especially that it was spoken by adults is that the snake might have been an ancestral spirit that came to check on the family. The Basubia had a mastery of controlling or working well with wild animals from long ago. This is tough for somebody to understand who is not of the tribe.

THE LION BIDDER

My late grandfather, Mbeha Masene, once told me of a man during his boyhood years that had an ability to communicate and give orders to lions. We are a people that traditionally employ wild plants and concoctions to our advantage. Different concoctions were used for different purposes. Even now there are those that have the ability to punish their enemies by means of lightening. The lightening would only strike its target from a group of people and leave innocent people uninjured.

Then there are those that had control over pythons and other venomous snakes. I know you do not believe it. Maybe you need to spend a year living in a purely Basubia village to understand. Thieves couldn't enter the field of someone that used snakes or lightening. Such people are said to have 'drunk' the animal or the rain in our culture. When they die, the object that they had *drunk* has to bid the family farewell. Or it may show up unexpectedly after a long time.

The man that my grandfather told me about was called Vasha Kavata, a direct relation of mine. He had a stray cow that always troubled him more than the rest. It preferred not to spend the night inside the kraal. By sleeping outside the kraal it attracted attention from the cattle that were inside the kraal. Eventually they would jump out through the acacia branches that hedged them from danger to join Lyambai, for so it was called. Vasha Kavata didn't like waking up from his sleep to go and drive the cattle that had got out of the kraal at the influence of Lyambai. Lyambai's behavior became established. One day its owner spoke to it as though he was speaking to a person, like one on one, face to face, giving it a warning that one day it would regret its actions but it would be too late to do anything about it.

'*Ka o hitirire mulyango lomuvi lozuva. Ici cintu cako ci ca kula ahulu.*' He had said in Subia. 'One day you will miss the entrance. Your behavior has gone out of hand.' Then one evening after supper time, when everyone was inside the reed compound, they heard animals running outside. From analysis it looked like there were three animals outside, and one of them was being chased. They couldn't see what was going on outside because it had become dark and also due to the tall reeds that enclosed them in from seeing outside.

He said that they saw something that looked like a shadow fly above the compound, followed by another swift movement of an animal that they did not recognize. Dust arose. They began to choke as a result. A single loud mournful sound was heard in front of the compound. Everything went silent after that. Vasha Kavata was the first to rise up and open the door of the reed wall. Lyambai lay motionlessly in front of the compound. At a short distance from her were two lionesses laying down on their bellies like well trained dogs waiting for their master to tell them what to do next. The lionesses had killed the cow, and could not eat it because they were not ordered to do so. Lyambai's master spoke to it again even in its death. '*Niva ku lwiri.*' 'I told you.' The cow had died from its stubbornness; the death could have been avoided. The wild beasts never tasted even an aota of Lyambai's blood. The old man thanked them for a job well done and ordered them to return to the wild again. They rose up when he spoke those words and left.

Lyambai's carcass spent the whole night at the spot it was killed at until sunrise. In the morning they skinned it and ate the meat. Everything went back to normal after that.

There was another day that Vasha Kavata's powers were manifested again. He and my grandfather had a trip to make to Ngweze from Linyanti village on Saturday night. He called the two same lionesses on a Tuesday night to come to the village. After supper, the people that were inside the compound heard some roars that neared with every heartbeat. The creatures stopped in front of the compound. He went out to commune with them. 'On Saturday evening we are going to Ngweze. Please come here on time so that we do not delay in setting off. Thank you for coming, you can go back now.'

At exactly the appointed time, four days after, the approaching lions made their presence felt by roaring as they neared the village. The young men went out to yoke the oxen together for the trip. There were no vehicles then. When everything was ready, he beckoned the ferocious beasts to start off. They walked at a great distance in front of the yoke of oxen. They reached

Ngweze safely that night without encountering any dangerous wild animal. No hyena or other lions dared get closer because they saw that there were lions in front of them that went on roaring.

On a day that they were to return to Linyanti, the lions showed up again. They never came late for their summons. Vasha Kavata decided to linger in Ngweze a bit longer. Since he wasn't going to be joining them, he gave them a pot that contained concoctions. He told them to open it and make it face the opposite direction that they were coming from. The pot was meant to send the scent of the oxen in an opposite direction, making it hard for other predators to trouble them.

They arrived safely at the village in the early hours of the morning, without meeting any dangerous animal.

MUM AND THE ELEPHANT

Kasane is a very small town geographically and in population. There are only two Primary Schools, and one Junior Secondary School. There is no High School in town and in the entire district; our children have to travel 300km to complete their Secondary School education; that is Grade 11 and 12. We have more Safari Lodges than clinics or shopping malls.

The town is well known for the famous Chobe River and the Chobe National Park that is home to the largest world elephant population. There are more elephants than people. Over the years, the town has experienced some difficulty in geographical extension to accommodate its growth. On the north of the town, there is the Chobe River that serves as the boundary line between Botswana and Namibia. On the west is the Chobe National Park. On the south lies a forest reserve. Finally on the east is an animal corridor that animals use when they are coming from the forest to the river. There is not much free land.

Like any town there are certain pieces of land in it that are not developed. The largest undeveloped area is the one that lies between the Plateau and down town Kasane. It has been a bush for a long time. The Elephants, Cape Buffaloes and Lions use it to cross from the Chobe National Park on the west to the eastern part of town. Elephants like to use and feed on this part of Kasane because the trees are not destroyed like some in the

National Park. They fancy the trees here as there is no competition from other animals. Buffaloes use it as an escape route from the lions that seek to kill them. The area is not entirely safe at any time of the day.

You may ask how we survive. Well, we have learnt to accept the situation. Kasane is an economic area for most of our people. The lodges employ more people than any sector of the town's economy. I guess we have accepted the life. This does not imply that we totally enjoy it. Of cause we love it here; we are so blessed and greatly privileged to live in an area that most people are dreaming of. The majority of Batswana have never visited the town; they only see it on television. It is like a miniature paradise. But there are consequences that come with this life that are rarely known to the tourist that sleeps in a five star hotel, and has a three course meal at the end of the day. Fish from the Chobe River is our staple food; we can eat it daily and feel like we haven't eaten fish before.

My mother lives on the plateau, on a higher elevation than the main CBD. The location she lives in is also called Plateau. She has been living there for the past fifteen years. Her workplace is a few kilometers down town at Kasane Industrial site. To get to her place of work she either walks or boards a taxi. A few years ago the government used to transport its employees with a government bus to and from work every day. That has stopped and civil servants have to find means of how they get to work. The only civil servants that are still transported to work every morning and afternoon by government bus are the Wildlife officers; their offices are in the bush.

One morning as usual, my mother left her house ten minutes after seven in the morning to walk to work. Normally she walked twenty minutes from home to work. She descended the plateau with two of her lady friends using a wide sandy road that went past the Zion Christian Church. The road they used is a good short cut for any person in a hurry, and it was more favorable for her considering where she was staying. Residents of the town that were born in any part of the district, like walking from one end of town to the next, instead of using public transport within town. This has probably been influenced by them spending most of their life in town and seeing it grow.

As is common to women, they talked of various subjects as they walked that road. With no prior warning a raging elephant appeared about ten meters in front of them. The space between them and the elephant was too small. They all turned around 360^0 to run. Mum was the oldest in the group, in her late fifties. The two young women managed to out run her. When she looked back she saw that the elephant had closed the gap. She saw it raise its trunk. Intuitively she felt something telling her to through away her sling bag and then throw herself to the ground. Immediately she threw the sling bag away from her, the elephant snatched it in midair not letting it touch the ground. She threw herself to the ground, missing a powerful blow from the elephant's trunk. It wanted to hit her with its truck; thank God for saving her and she fell down at the very time that the elephant wanted to squash the life out of her. Falling down she rolled into the shrubs that were nearby, her clothes being torn in the process. The furious elephant looked for her all over, it madly wanted her.

Her friends who had managed to run away were crying uncontrollably thinking that it had finished her up. One of the ladies originated from south of Botswana she was not Chobean. They were so scared, shaking, confused, shocked, and not knowing what to do. 'Oh, it has killed her. It has killed her.'

By the grace of God my mother survived. The elephant didn't find her. She got up, with a dizzy mind. Not knowing where to run to, she ran in any direction. Unbeknown to her, she was running towards the direction that her friends had run to. Her skirt was torn, her eye glasses were lost and the phone was nowhere to be found.

They went back home, to mum's place, all of them. At home they tried to get hold of the wildlife officers, a task they had difficulty achieving. Only a concerned friend is the one that managed to help them out by contacting the wildlife authorities, it is interesting that they were called by somebody who was out of town.

When they arrived, they took the three women with them to go and show them where they had met the elephant. Mum sat in the cabin of the government Toyota Land Cruiser with one officer, the other officer was at the back in the open. The elephant spotted them; it made its way towards them. What a day this was . . . the game ranger who was at the back of the car had left his gun next to where mum was seated. The animal came charging with all rage that it had to display. It was chaos. By this time it was the elephant against the vehicle. The man at the back managed to get the gun to his side. The soldiers also arrived on the scene.

The two vehicles moved into all directions. Dust was all over the place. With a struggle they managed to shoot it.

It is customary that a dangerous animal is killed before it could kill any person. After it has been killed, its carcass is left for the community members to eat. Everybody flocked to where it had died some with axes and wheel barrows, all in the name of free meat. Life is so funny, the elephant wanted to kill my mother; instead it is the one that got killed and some of the local residents were fighting to get a piece of its meat. They didn't care whether it had intended to kill somebody or not, all they wanted was the meat. People can really be strange.

I got to know five hours after the incidence through a phone call from my cousin who wanted to know what had exactly happened. I had no idea what she was talking about. Guess how shocked I was. I called mum, only to find that it was true. I would have lost my mother five hours ago on that day, April 6th 2010. Whenever I think of this incidence my emotions are raised and I get filled with anger, not to anybody in particular but to the elephant. Whenever I see any elephant, I think of what it nearly did to my mother. When everybody is smiling and wishing to take a picture of the elephant or of coming to Chobe to see elephants, I curse the animal.

Perils of Tranquility

I am mum's youngest son, I have two elder brothers. No sister. I love my mother a lot, that is why when I think of what nearly happened that morning my feelings get mixed up. The three women were very fortunate to have survived the attack. I do not recall of any incidence in our area that somebody had survived an elephant attack.

A number of years ago, our neighbor at the cattle post got killed by an elephant right on the spot. He had a gun with him; it broke the gun to pieces and stepped on his chest. He had tried to run, but in vain. Another man in Mabele village, near Kavimba, was killed by an elephant between 3pm and 4pm in the afternoon when he was in the ranches heading cattle. The elephant had found him sleeping under a tree since it was hot. It pierced him with one of its tasks on the chest. That was the end of him. His next waking moment will be in eternity. He did not hear the elephant coming, it walks so silently. I try to put myself in his position. He was not prepared. What a way of dying.

In 2001, another man was killed between Kasane and Kazungula. He was originally from Tutume village, near the city of Francistown. He had been warned by residents of Kazungula not to try his luck by walking the 9 kilometers from Kazungula to Kasane. He did not take heed of the warning. When he reached Chobe Farms he was ambushed by an elephant. He had not seen it. It made him fall to the ground, pressed one of its tasks through his chest, and then lifted him up, suspended on the task and threw him away. He did not fall far from where it was. By an act of providence, two police officers who happened to be driving past on the road saw the elephant and could tell from its behavior that something unusual was happening. They saw the man lying helplessly next to the road, struggling to contain his fleeting life within him. He was rushed to the hospital. His wounds were so severe it needed a bigger hospital. The referral hospital is in Francistown, five hours drive on tarred road. The man could not make it in those five hours. He died at the airport before being flown away.

Three months after my mother's incidence, somebody I know, a relation was attacked by an elephant in Mavere. He died a cruel and miserable death. He breathed his last around 2pm on a warm winter afternoon. After killing him it hanged him between branches of a nearby tree with the blood of his lifeless form flowing to the ground. What a terrible sight.

As if that is not enough, last week Wednesday, two months after he died somebody got killed again by an elephant in Kazungula. I am not certain if any of the elephants that killed these people who died untimely deaths were tracked down and shot. I doubt that they were found.

There are also people in town who have been killed by cape buffalos and only a few have survived their attacks. Some years back when I was still a student of Chobe Junior Secondary School, there was a man who was attacked by a buffalo on the same road that my mum met the elephant. He was not as fortunate as my mother was. It ripped open his tummy exposing the intestines with its horns and left him to die. He died on the spot.

A certain fuel attendant was once run into by a buffalo on one early winter morning on his way to work, from Plateau down town. It was before 6am, and it was still dark. The buffalo hit him at a place that is commonly known in town as 'the stairs'; there are fifty four concrete stairs from below up the plateau that are used by people to descend and ascend depending on where they are headed. By then the District Council had not installed spot lights along the street lights on the pathway. The young man never saw the buffalo. He was in a hurry to report for duty before 6am and not be late.

When he regained consciousness he did not recognize his surroundings. He lay down motionlessly on the ground after he had been knocked down. Somebody who came that way saw him on the ground; he called the police who took him to the hospital. The buffalo was lenient on him.

Another lady, on the same road that my mother had used that morning was chased by a buffalo two or three years ago. It was after 16:30hours and a number of people were on their way home up the plateau. I think it was during the month of July. A group of ladies were walking together. Among them was a lady who was carrying a baby on her back. Out of nowhere a buffalo came into their sight. They all ran. The mother with a baby on her back forgot that she was carrying a baby. She untied the wrapper and put the baby down then ran for her life. There are some mothers who are like that you know. Mothers that can run away and leave their babies exposed to danger. One of the women in the group became the main target of the buffalo. It had singled her out from the rest and it ran after her.

She looked back; saw that the buffalo was less than two meters from her. She threw herself down. It missed her. There is a commonly accepted theory that the buffalo closes its eyes before attacking somebody, I do not know how true the theory is, but I will not dare prove it. If the theory or belief is true, when the buffalo opened its eyes it couldn't see the woman.

She got up and ran towards the Zion Christian Church that is on the low land. There she was found by the wildlife authorities who helped her get her phone back by ringing it. The mother who had out of fear been coward enough to save her life by leaving her infant at the mercy of the animal managed to get her child back.

Well, I know you might be asking yourself what is the price of life. What do victims get for compensation from the government for sustaining wounds or losing their lives? Or if they die in the process what compensation does the family have. My answer is nothing in the form of money. Life has no price in monetary terms. They will get recognition in the evening at 18:10 hours by national extra news bulletin coverage. Beyond that they get nothing. Life returns to how it has been; it is business as usual like some would say. My mother got nothing in the form of money. There is no price to life.

I thought I had got used to this kind of life; of dying any minute like flies, without being given a notice. But I have not. I become emotional when I think of all these situations. Should I blame God, or my parents for having born me into this place, or should I blame the government? No, I blame nobody; everything has consequences, good and bad. That is the nature of life, it is never fair. Even the richest people are not safe. Unfortunately for us there is nowhere we can run to, this is home. We have to go through this kind of life, of animals killing us; while they are prized above our lives.

"The dangers of life are infinite, and among them is safety" Goethe. I guess he should have said 'the dangers of life are infinite, and among them is *beauty.*' It would make a lot of sense in this situation.

THE LIONS OF PANDAMATENGA

Pandamatenga is a very deceptive village to the traveler. Many people on transit have often wondered where the village is actually located when they pass by. Shopping complexes, the silos, fuel stations, and commercial farms are the only things that are common sight. The entire village is hidden from 'public' view. From the main road to where I stay, it is a distance of approximately 6km. My house is about 300m from the Botswana—Zimbabwe boarder line. There is no electric fence or standard fence on the border line. Interestingly there are no cases of border jumpers or illegal immigrants. The city of Hwange is 80km East South on the Zimbabwean side, while Victoria falls is 100km north east.

The village is divided into three separate communities. Far on the south west are the commercial farms that are surrounded by an electric fence with a radius of over 40km, these farms play a very big role in providing the entire country with grains; sorghum, beans and sunflower. They are run by expatriates and citizens; we often call them professional farmers. Next comes a part of the village commonly known as 'Crasher' which in truth is 'Crusher'. The location got its name from long ago when there was a quarry where stones were crushed for making the Nata—Kazungula road. Guest House ward is the third and last part of the village. There is 4km of un-inhabited land between Crasher and Guest House.

Quite a number of people have been allocated residential plots by the Land Board, but there are relatively few people that have built their plots. Most of them are afraid of staying alone in the 'bush' as they say. So they are waiting for their neighbors to first build and move in to their built plots, that is when they can build too.

Every day after sunset there are no pedestrians that can be seen walking from Crasher to Guest House or from Guest House to Crasher. Those who dare walk do so in large numbers; mostly going to the bars and back again when the bars close at 22:00hours or an hour before midnight during weekends.

There are lions that frequent the un-inhabited land at night, especially at the stream where there are seven culverts. Here some wells have been dug out by cattle owners. The trees are of massive height and it is scary to walk past this area at night. If a person who stays in Guest House arrives late at night or before sunrise by the Lusaka bus from Gaborone—Francistown or anywhere in the country, that person will have to take refuge at the Police Station in Crasher until sunrise, or until the police officers feel pity for them by driving them home when they go out on their patrols.

On January 18th 2010 the lions attacked my neighbor's cattle at 3am. On that night I was sleeping in the spare bedroom, I wanted to sleep on the floor and not on the bed. I liked the spare bedroom since its windows were facing the east and one could easily enjoy the morning sunlight and the breeze that comes from the eastern sky. I woke up from my sleep, lifted my head from the pillow to listen attentively to the sound outside the house. I heard something running in the stillness of the night. I heard it increase speed. I knew without the shadow of a doubt what it was. A lion had paid us a visit. There is a gravel road that lies between me and my neighbor, after her house is a bush that extends towards the border line.

Like a gushing wind it charged. Grrrrrrrrr!!!!!!!!!!!!!! I froze, no movement as if it was inside the house. The cattle went hysterical, got out of the kraal and ran for 'safety' in all directions. Stupid animals, by getting out of the kraal they thought they were running away from the lion to safety while the opposite was true. The charging lion did not get inside the kraal; they rarely get in the kraal. They scare the cattle by charging, running as if they are going to jump into the kraal. By the time they get near, all the cattle out of fear would have jumped outside to danger thinking they were not safe in the kraal. Three of them ran past my house into the interior of the village. Some ran towards Zimbabwe, the rest I do not know where they ran.

'Mogolo, Mogolo . . . . Mogolo' the old woman who is my neighbor shouted out the cattle keeper's name. She called out again 'Mogolo, Mogolo, Mogolo . . . .' No answer. I wouldn't have answered if she had called my name. What had attacked were lions, not dogs. There is a big difference between the two. She called for Mogolo so that she would give him the gun to shoot them. Why did she keep the gun in the first place when she could not use it? She is not the only one of her age group who liked keeping the gun, knowing she could not use it in times of danger. My grandmother liked doing the same.

She kept shouting out his name. He could hear her, but did not answer. Finally I managed to master the strength to get up. I switched on the outside light on the veranda in time to see three cattle run in front of my house. I didn't get out of the house; I saw them through the window. An ox and a calf that had ran into the bush were killed before leaving the country. Wildlife authorities arrived at 7:30 am, long after the lions were gone. Here is the interesting thing, the lions came through from Zimbabwe and returned after their kill. Our wildlife officers could not follow them into Zimbabwe; they needed special permission to do that. These beasts know that there is safety on the Zimbabwean side. On the other side of the border line is the Matetsi Hunting Area, South of it is the Hwange National Park. 30km north of Matetsi Hunting area is the Kazuma National park. So the lions were totally safe.

The dead ox was found that morning. It had been wasted; no meat was eaten except the intestines, and left for whatever would care to eat. The owner was compensated, less than P500.00, which is almost US$80.00. Had she been the one to sell her ox while it was alive she would have got six times that amount.

The following night they attacked 100m from my neighbor's kraal. They killed three of her cattle. Two big ones and a small calf. Gloria, the owner, woke up that early morning and walked a kilometer to the Wildlife office to lodge a complaint. She did not wait for daylight nor did she care that she would meet with a lion. She was so bold, and the game authorities came back with her that very night. They took her statement; unfortunately the harm had already been done.

A few days ago I had the privilege of listening to Mama Gladys tell me about the beautiful puppy that she found in her yard one early morning when she woke up.

She was sleeping with her daughter Gladys in the single hut that they have in their residential plot. That night she had a dream of a lioness training its two cubs. In her dream she saw the lioness and the cubs coming from the forest and sleeping in front of her house. She was scared for Gladys as they did not have a toilet in the house. She woke up from her dream and was excited that it was only a dream. When they got outside the house with the first rays of the sun, they saw that there was a strangely beautiful puppy in their compound. It was admirable. Gladys wanted to hold it. Unfortunately it kept going further from her. She got irritated of the stubborn beautiful puppy. Both Mama Gladys and Gladys started throwing stones at the puppy. Each time she threw a stone close to it; it would show off its teeth and make a funny noise. They threw more stones. A neighbor found them throwing stones at it. She was speechless at what they were doing. She said "Do you know what you people are doing? This is not a puppy it's a cub, it is a small lion. The mother may not be far from here. The lioness may appear anytime." The cub ran off to the forest, probably to its mother. A few minutes later their other neighbor came from the side of the cattle kraal. He was tracking a lioness and its two cubs that had been at his kraal that very night. The tracks led to Mama Gladys kraal. It seemed that the lioness was training its cubs on how to hunt for themselves. He found where the beasts and its cubs had laid down in front of the kraal. They didn't attack the cattle. They lay down in front of the kraal and got up to leave before sunrise. Somehow the cub remained behind and that is how they found it in their compound when they woke up.

A week ago a certain farmer was driving late in the evening to his farm. His van got stuck in the mud as it had rained heavily during the day. So when he failed to free his vehicle from the mud, he decided to walk a distance of a kilometer to the nearest farm to get help. Upon coming back, he heard a lion and a lioness roaring near his van. He made a u-turn and headed back to where he was coming from. Scared for his life, wondering what would have happened if the lions had seen him before he saw them. He did not have a gun with him or anything to defend himself with.

With the help of the neighbors they managed to free the vehicle, enabling him to get home around 3am.

Although he was scared at the time, he was content that they have never attacked his cattle. They always pass his kraal at night.

6

BORDER PYTHON

This python was found in a chicken cage in one of the households at the back of the village towards the border line. It had been a dark rainy night, and I went to bed early. My cousin went out with two boys accompanying them to their home. It seems the boys had spent most of the day playing and they forgot to go home before sunset. That is why he decided to accompany them, and then he would bring the other safely to his home. First they began by going to the home that was far off. My words to him as they left were 'be careful of the road you are going to be using. There are snakes where you are going.'

He got back and we slept. Unbeknown to us, that at the very home he had been to, would be killed this python.

As it was raining it got into the chicken cage and began swallowing chickens. Mama Morwa kept reminding the children to close the chicken cage. Her young sister went out to close it. After she closed them in, she saw a log that seemed to be moving inside the cage. The chickens were running all over the place. She asked somebody to bring some light so that they would see what was happening. Lo and behold, it was a python over 3meters in length. It had already eaten some chickens. One of them rushed to the Wildlife camp so that they would come and kill. I'm told they shot it four times before it died. They took it away with them.

Interesting enough there are some people around who eat it. It eats people and people also eat it.

Later in the morning some men came to skin it. The skin is often taken by the government and the men have the meat. I watched them skin it, and remove the two chickens that it had swallowed. I didn't see any meaty parts on its long body; it was all white meat with bones all the way.

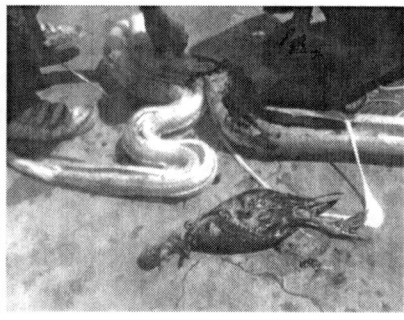

It was not the first python that was killed inside a chicken cage. Mma Marry once found it in her chicken cage a few years ago. She had heard that chickens were under attack. Her son went out with a touch to check on what had attacked them. He got scared when he saw it and never said a word to his mother. Early morning he went to work without telling others what he had seen. The mother went out to check on the cage before leaving for work. She found its head outside the cage, through the mesh wire. The whole body had gotten too big to come out through the same way it had gone into the cage. It was full of eating many chickens, and its body couldn't let it leave the cage. She went behind the cage and pricked it on the tail. Then it reversed into the cage, and aligned itself with some poles that were lying down. Probably the idea was to fool anyone who would come around into thinking it was a log. The only difference is that its body was very big from the chickens it had swallowed. She hit its head several times, so that it started vomiting them out. By the time that the Wildlife authorities arrived, it was already dead.

Both of these pythons came in through the side of the Zimbabwean border.

7
GAME WARDENS

Poha Wildlife camp is located in the heart of Chobe National Park. The only people who live there are game wardens and soldiers, mostly occupying tents.

I heard of three game wardens that were warming themselves by a camp fire one night. They had already eaten their supper. Then one of them rose up to pour out water. Upon turning his back to the darkness a lion got up at terrible speed charging at him from the darkness. The other men who were seated at the fire got up too and ran to the safety of their tents.

Dead silence followed afterwards when each of them was in the safety of their tents. The pulse of each of them beat faster through the night. None knew who had survived until sunrise. It was every man for himself and God for them all.

I heard of other game wardens who had camped somewhere in the National Park. Among them was a man who isolated himself from the rest, pitching his tent at a distance. His colleagues occupied a building. He took his small tent and pitched it on top of a water pipe line. The pipe had a small leak underneath. I suspect he pitched the tent at night, as he did not see that the ground upon which he pitched his tent was moist. At night when they were asleep, elephants began pouring into the camp. One of the elephants detected the scent of moist soil and decided to follow the trail. It started going along the pipe line, digging underneath it for traces of water as it was thirsty. It got to the tent. Its four legs were around the tent. The man inside the tent woke up and realized what was going on outside. He dared not make any sound. Stealthily, he got his knife and truck keys. He waited for the elephant to scratch the ground again and simultaneously cut open the tent. This way the elephant could not detect that there was somebody in the tent. When he had made a gap that was wide enough, he took a deep breath, tore it wide open, and dashed out to the truck that was parked at a distance. The elephant saw something coming from underneath it. It gave out a loud trumpet noise while circling around trying to make sense of what was happening. By this time, the man was underneath the truck taking advantage of the darkness. Upon realizing that the elephant was still confused, he unlocked the truck and roared the engine of the truck to life.

The elephant had become hysterical. It tore the tent to pieces. His colleagues got their guns out and shot it. That was the only thing they could do to ensure that their stay was safe although they are paid to protect and care for wild animals.

The elephant had taught the man the worst thing about isolating himself from others. Unity and sticking together is important for any group of people that have a similar mission.

8
XAXABA

My uncle told me of an incident that happened when he was still working at Xaxaba camp on the east of the Okavango Delta. One of his colleagues who was a Professional Guide had a girlfriend in Seronga village, 4km from the camp. Between Xaxaba and Seronga there was uninhabited bush. Tom, as he was called, decided one night to go and check on his girlfriend at the village. He snuck out of the camp alone and braved the dark night. He reached his lover and spent a few hours in her bosom. At 4am, he traced his steps back to camp.

When he had covered half the distance to camp, alone like before, he heard a noise that scared him, 'boggggg!!!!!!' He fell to the ground and began shouting out for his mum to come help him. His mother was nowhere near him. Even if she was close to him, she would not have risked coming out in the darkness to him.

Tom did heavily sweat. He lay down there thinking that he was being eaten by a lion. I guess he had lost all hope and must have been too scared even to feel his flesh being ripped apart by the teeth of the king of the forest. I can picture him feeling like he had reached heaven, for that is where most people think they go when they die.

Nobody ever came to him help. As the first rays of the sun were breaking through the eastern skies, he opened his eyes. Surprisingly he was still alive and in good shape. There were marks on the ground, showing how much he had kicked thinking that he was caught by a lion. He got up and began moving forward. A few feet from him he saw Kudu tracks. A kudu is a type of an antelope. He had not been scared by a lion. Instead it seems he had caught a kudu off guard and it ran out to safety while he fell to the ground and screamed for his life. Never again in his life has he gone out to visit a girlfriend in the night far from where he stays.

On a certain morning, Presley and two other tour guides rolled their three wooden canoes, mokoros, into the stream that was in front of their camp. Each guide had some tourists with him in his mokoro. They lined up as they moved on the waters, with Presley leading the way. For no apparent reason he let his colleagues paddle past him and he followed from behind.

The man in front of the line touched a hippo with his long wooden paddle. He did not realize that he had pushed his wooden paddle against the back of a hippo that was down in the water. Enraged, the hippo emerged colliding with the second mokoro that was in the line. It hit it with great force, breaking it to pieces and sending both the Professional Guide and his clients into the air. None of them expected what happened. Both the men who were in front and behind froze. There was nothing they could do to help the victims of the attack.

Fortunately everybody who was in the mokoro that was broken to pieces knew how to swim. Thus they managed to swim to safety before the hippo got any of them.

Following this incident, Presley resigned from mokoro safaris, and there was no mokoro activity for that day. The juices and alcohol at the hotel could not calm the clients. It was an experience they would remember for as long as they lived.

9
A NIGHT IN THE FOREST

Mbanga Shamukuni

In 1998, we drove out our six oxen through the forest to graze and to drink water at Lungara. At that time we kept oxen for farming our fields at Kavimba, we did not have cows.

It was customary that during the rainy season we would drive our cattle through the forest as there were various plants that the cattle could feed upon. Our forest has elephants, lions, buffaloes, kudus, zebras, hyenas, giraffes, wildebeests, cheetahs and leopards. There are a lot of animals that live in the forest. We share the forest with these animals. During the day they do not come close to our homes that are lined along the river front. At night they come much closer.

Growing up in our environment made us brave. Moving through the forest daily while heading cattle had become a way of living for us. One morning, I went out with my cousin Muhinda Kakambi. He was only 11 years old at the time. In our times he was of age to herd cattle through the forest. The boy could spend the whole day without eating and could walk about 10km daily with the cattle. We drove the cattle from our kraal and led them south east into the forest via an area in the forest that had once become a timber factory in the late 1980s. The ruins to the timber factory are located inside a valley, but there is plenty of open space around it. There is also a borehole. After reaching the timber factory, we turned north and rose up out of the valley to appear on the plains of Lungara, where there was a Police Station servicing the entire five Chobe Enclave villages. Normally it took us about four hours to reach the river at Lungara from home. England is the name that cattle herders gave to the river front at Lungara. I have no idea why it is called England. It has lots of fish and there is a hippo that can even be found there.

Our cattle drank water and we spent about an hour at Lungara before we headed back home through the same route we had come. In going back, we endeavored to hasten our pace so that we would not meet elephants and other animals towards sunset. We set out facing south west climbing up the plateau. How we lost our coordinates is a mystery to this day. As we descended the plateau into the valley that would lead us to the old timber factory we turned cattle eastwards in a wrong direction, thinking it was the way home. The cattle inclined in a direction that we should have been going. Since we are their masters, they went our direction after much effort.

I wondered why on this particular day it took us a long time to reach home. The vegetation and soil began changing. Our soil is reddish sand and the vegetation in the forest reserve near Kavimba has a lot of Zambezi teak (Mokusi) and other trees. The soil we were treading upon was white sand and there were plenty of mopane trees. This was enough to tell us that we were lost. The sun began sinking low in the western skies. Fortunately I had some match sticks, a short gun, and seven bullets. We spotted a tree that had a big trunk with a hollow that Muhinda could fit in. The tree had to serve as Muhinda's bedroom for the night. We lit fire and the oxen stopped moving. They lay down on the ground close to us. I told Muhinda to climb up the tree while I kept watch on the ground the whole night. Had it not been for the help of my wrist watch the night would have been much longer. A hyena kept bothering us but it did not come any closer. For the first time in my life I heard a leopard's call. Since a leopard is smaller in size than a cow it had no ability of killing any of them.

At home they led out a search party for us after darkness. The police were also involved and they went out through different bands. One of the search bands targeted Tinto cattle post which is a distance from the plains. The gun shots that they made went unheard since we were far in the forest. I kept checking my time; 1am, 3am, 5am, and 6am. By the way, we had made an arrow on the ground the previous night on the direction we were headed, so that we do not lose our way. But we were already lost, and the arrow pointed us further in the opposite direction. We followed the direction of the arrow, to appear from the South western part of Mabele village after sun rise. We recognized where we were by now. So we went down the main road that is 10km to Kavimba. I had not lost the guinea fowl that I had killed the previous afternoon. All attention was on us. Those at home told us what they went through during the night while searching for us.

The experience taught us and many others that cattle and other domestic livestock rarely lose their way home. They know how to find their way even when the masters are lost.

I wonder how it would have been like if I had no match sticks or a gun.

10

THE WRATH OF THE ZAMBEZI RAPIDS

Morgan Ncube

My brother Diro is a guide working for a rafting company in Victoria Falls. I always wondered what he meant when he said rafting is different every day. Every morning when he wakes up, he is always undecided whether to go to work or not, yet he is the most paid worker in our family. I always tell him to get used to his job. The Zambezi rapids are something you can never get used to because it is a different experience every day of the year.

Rafting is done in the Zambezi River just below the famous Victoria Falls in Zimbabwe. There are four different companies doing rafting within this river. Diro works for Shearwater Rafting Company. When business is low, the company invites people from other different companies as a means of marketing itself. Opportunity strikes and I get invited to prove why my brother never gets used to his job yet he has been working at the same company for the past decade. He books me for Saturday November 30th.

It is a warm day, and the best day of the year for me because it is a day when Diro and I are going to work for the same company. He seems excited. He is determined to prove his point that the Zambezi rafting experience is not only different daily, but every hour as well.

We arrive at the registration point where every client is required to sign an indemnity form. It clearly states 'that in case of DEATH and the like,' (the word death is written in capital letters so that everybody can read it); 'the company is NOT in any position to compensate.'

Business is so low for this rafting company today. My brother proposes to book me for two days. I am very fortunate. I do not even ask whether the bookings have been approved or not. I think they have been approved because I get to sign two indemnity forms, one for Saturday and the other for Sunday. Then we walk to a further point where we meet a River Guide who takes us through the Safety Talk.

"Welcome to the mighty Zambezi River Spectacular, my name is Guy and I am your guide for the day. I will take you through the Safety Talk and I would like to know from you what you will like me to begin with, either the good news or the bad news about the Zambezi river."

The majority vote for the bad news first. Then he said, "You have all signed your indemnity form and have seen the word DEATH on it. Yes rafting is one such experience where you have both fun and death in one. There are eleven rapids altogether. At each rapid you will experience a different episode, from easy ride to extremely dangerous which we have come to describe as Commercial Suicide." He paused as though to confirm that everyone had heard clearly. "Hold on very tightly to the rope on your rafts at this rapid" pointing to a map on a large board, "at this point you will certainly flip off your rafts. If you happen to sink deep down the water, remember not to scream, because I promise you no matter how loud you may scream no one will hear you under water." He nodded with his head to emphasis that there will be nobody to hear anybody screaming deep inside the river. "The rafter is an egg shaped inflated tube that will keep you floating for the next 11km from this point. Do not ask me to stop it down the rapids because neither does it have brakes nor has any company on this river ever produced a guide who can stop it." One woman among the clients exclaimed, 'Oh that is quite a record!' He looked at her for a while and said, "I have been working on this river for the past decade and I am one of those who cannot stop the raft half way down the rapid. I am not ashamed to say so. And now for the good news, we are a big company and we have no DEATH record yet." He said the word DEATH as though still writing it with capital letters. "I promise you that we will all come out of this river alive and ascend the hundred and twenty steps up the Zambezi gorges, which is one of the Bad Safety talks that I forgot to tell you about and the same distance you are going to descend after this talk. Are we all ready to start the trip?"

Everybody said yes except for one army commander who looked unmoved by what the guide had said. Guy spotted him and immediately said "Sir, are you ready for the adventure or have you decided otherwise?" He laughed out loud enough to put courage on everyone who was quiet, including me. "I am more than ready and I think my junior lady soldiers are ready too. I am their

Perils of Tranquility

army commander. They are here to prove their fitness to me." I was standing next to him and his physical fitness told me that he was right. He was muscular and poised as a sentinel.

The guide continued "Then we are all set to go. Oh! By the way, we are going to take our lunch half way through our ride so that everyone will be having enough energy to climb the set of steps out of the gorge. No one has ever failed to make it outside the gorge before, except for one old woman who had a fractured leg two years ago. However, we have very strong potters at the end of the trip. Should you fail to make it up the stairs, please do not be afraid to ask them to carry you on their backs. The little steps in front of you will lead you to the bottom of the river where three rafts are waiting to take you through the day."

He motioned the other guide to lead the way down the gorge. Half way down, my legs started shaking and the river that had looked small from above now looked very big and impossible to raft on its waters.

Once we arrived at the bottom of the gorge, we came together and the guide continued to take us through the safety talk again. Showing clients how to tighten their Safety jackets that can enable us to keep floating on top of the water, he proceeded to the safety kayaks that other guides will use to escort to the medical box that they always carry on the journey in case there is anyone who bleeds from hitting the rocks. He finally informed us about the video camera that will be accompanying us, in the care of other guides in the safety kayaks. The video was to capture the moments we were going to have in the river and then produce the video for our own benefit.

Finally they placed us in groups of six in each raft. I was so pleased to realize that I was placed in the same raft with the proud army commander and two of his lady soldiers. "The river runs in a zigzag pattern. At every corner we have a rapid that you will only be able to see when you are two meters away. This is an advantage for us otherwise we will have people falling out of the raft before we get to it." We all laughed as Guy concluded his talk before we tested the waters. He asked my brother to lead the group. We were in the middle.

I could hear the sound of the rolling water grow as we neared the first raft. Those in the raft ahead of us could be heard screaming, we passed it easily without any one falling out of the raft. Guy informed us that the next two rapids were going to be similar to the one that we just went past. The fourth raft was named Commercial Suicide. Commercial Suicide was much louder. A certain lady on the raft that was before us shouted, 'stop this thing. I can't make it ...' before she could say more words she found herself in the water and was washed away like a leaf that is carried away by a strong current of water. The army commander gave out a hearty laughter and encouraged his juniors to be brave.

My heart beat doubled as we approached the dreaded rapid. I recalled what was said during the Safety talk. Death was closing in on us. The raft hit head on the rapid and folded in and stretched out quickly throwing everyone up into the air. I saw the army commander fly past me and land heavily into the rapid. I held tight to the rope on the boat, until I got past the rapid and Guy, the guide, pulled me back into the boat. The Commander was trapped in the rapid and was popping in and out, upside down. He finally floated past us quickly. Guy peddled the boat behind him trying to catch up with the man that was being carried away by the powerful water current. We had all managed to get in the boat except for him. Finally we caught up with him and we pulled him into the raft.

As he sighed with relief to finally be in the boat, I also sighed with surprise after I realized that his loins were completely not covered. Only the life jacket remained on him. He did not notice that he was naked. "You were the longest swimmer," Guy shouted. I kept my eyes on his naked buttocks. Everyone in the boat laughed except me. One lady soldier noticed and followed my stare; she was the second to notice "Oh my Gosh! Give him a towel." The army commander followed her gaze. He noticed and fell backwards into the water, then drifted away so fast by the current towards the boat that was in front of us. My brother who was the guide in that boat spotted him and moved the raft towards him to lend a helping hand. Diro caught the hand of the Army Commander and tried to pull him into the boat, but instead the Army Commander held onto the boat and pulled Diro into the water. We approached them with Guy who rescued the situation. He gave him a t-shirt and asked him to put it on up-side down, his legs coming out where the hands should have come out. Then he was pulled up into the boat. He looked so funny this time around that I too laughed.

He sat in the raft shivering. "Long swimmer" Guy shouted, "there will be a video show tonight about what just happened. You should call your wife to come and watch it. She can leave your children next door." The only people who laughed at hearing this were me and the guide. The commander was not happy to hear this, but Guy was right. There is a video show daily for every raft that takes place on that day, and clients can buy them if they wish. The commander finally found something to say. 'Is that what you kept saying by swimming when one is carried away by these dangerous waters? You white people are mad. You call DEATH fun! You call my nakedness funny!' He should not have mentioned nakedness because that word ignited more laughter from Guy and me.

We got to the point where we took a lunch break. As we ate, the commander was the talk of the hour. He had gained his composure and was apologizing to Guy for calling him a white person earlier on. Someone mentioned something about looking forward to watching the video that night, and so did I. One of the lady soldiers asked me if it was true there was going to be a video that night and I told her that it was not a joke. We made an appointment to meet at 7pm at the raft offices to watch the video. She was not certain if the commander would let them watch the video. As we took off for the remaining last half trip of the day, I kept looking at the commander who held tight to his rope even though the raft was cruising where the water was calm.

At the end of the raft, climbing up the gorge, my brother asked me if I would come again tomorrow. I answered him that I would come if more soldiers had booked. He asked me to arrange for a day off at work in order to be present the next day. There was not going to be any problems with me getting the day off from work, as I had more off days, and so Guy approved my attendance the following day since he was also the River Manager. 'You must come and watch the Zambezi Spectacular tonight,' Guy said once more to the Army Commander. 'I will buy the video for you as a gift for being one of the longest swimmers in my rafting carrier.' For the first time since the incident happened that day, the army commander laughed and asked Guy to stop saying funny things. Guy was right, rafting can be fun.

DAY II

I sat on top of the rock that my brother sat on the other day. We had already been separated into groups and introduced to our guides. Diro was going to be the man leading the way for our group.

As everybody signed the indemnity forms, I thought to myself that the one I had signed the previous day was still valid, but I was told that each day was a different day from other days. The forms were similar to yesterdays and the company emphasized that they will not be held liable for any DEATH that would occur. The word DEATH was in block letters as usual. Two lady clients from the USA and France refused to sign the form and had to return to their respective hotels.

'Hold on tight to your rope in the river.' One tall man who had watched the Zambezi Spectacular the previous night laughed and extended on the guide's words, 'otherwise the waters will undress you.'

Safety talk being done, we all descended the gorge to the rafts. I realized that I was put in the same group with the client who was making funny remarks about being undressed by the waters. He was physically strong and looked like he was ready to brave the mighty waters. 'I have done rafting before in the USA, but the river where I went did not have steep steps like this one,' He said without directing his speech to anyone in particular. Diro decided to open up a conversation with him. 'Rafting is different every time you go on the Zambezi River. No one knows the facts about our journey today; however, you have the choice to do half trip if you so feel.' 'I am not moved,' said the client. 'If ladies can do it, there is no way that I am going to chicken out. I want to be the first person to overcome the worst rapids and show the Army Commander that I am better than him when it comes to taming the wild river.' I envied his bravery and determination. When swimming was mentioned during the safety talk, I saw this particular client shift to the side a little and check his safety jacket. I figured out he was not a good swimmer.

Despite the fact that the first two rapids are easy rides, the American firmly held onto the rope. My brother had to tell him to loosen his grip after every rapid. He had to clap hands for the client to realize that he could take it easy.

We approached Commercial Suicide. The client looked at me and openly said, 'I am scared. I wish I did not take part in this.' I pitied him and assured him that I had gone

Perils of Tranquility

past that rapid the day before. 'We are getting closer to the biggest rapid in the river. Hold on to your rope, do not panic. This is Commercial Suicide.' The guide with the video camera stood on top of a rock. I waved at him and suddenly the raft started speeding into the rapid.

There is a curve known as the Devil's curve. Two big rocks stand erect next to each other and a small stream runs in between them. The space between the rocks is big enough to accommodate the legs only and not the whole body. All the guides who work for the company fear the Devil's curve, and my brother once told me about this curve before. He almost resigned from his job just because he nearly got stuck in the Devil's curve. I had encouraged him not to quit.

Our raft entered the Commercial suicide rapid. It spun around twice and a big wave hit us in our faces, partially rendering us blind. When I gained sight, I saw that the camera man was not pointing his camera at us. The camera was fixed on the Devil's curve. Shouting and clapping of hands came from the boat behind us. Our raft had gone past Commercial Suicide without capsizing. It was the second time in the history of the company for one of its rafts to pass Commercial Suicide without capsizing, and I was happy to be one of the passengers in this raft. I had made history. I raised my hand to shake my brother's, but before I said a word to him, I saw that his pupils were dilated and full of panic. I followed his gaze to the Devil's curve. It was until then that I noticed that we were one man short in our raft. His hand appeared once out of the curve as though to wave 'good bye.' We paddled to the bank of the river and watched what was happening on the rock where the cameraman stood perplexed. I could see the man struggling to set himself free. The orange colored life jacket could be seen underneath the water.

All the guides came to where we stood. They tried throwing a rope to him for him to cling onto it but he did not get it. Half an hour went by and there was no sign of the client. My brother looked at me and confirmed his usual speech that rafting was different every day. Guy organized all of us into using the two other rafts and we continued with the adventure. He assured us that they will finally rescue the client.

After all the clients had left, the oar that is normally used for controlling the raft was taken and used to push the client out. He rolled past us and no one asked whether he was alive or not, it was obvious that he was not alive. Diro took the raft and followed the corpse and pulled it to the edge of the river. The man appeared to have been dead for some time. His eyes were wide open. His body was wrapped in a plastic bag that is normally used for garbage. The body was tied to our raft and followed us like a trailer. Guess whose body it was; the tall man who had done rafting before in the United States of America.

It is believed that there is a big snake in the river called Nyami-nyami. One is not supposed to despise the Zambezi Rapids otherwise Nyami-nyami will not be happy with the despiser. After seeing what happened to the Army Commander and the client that lost his life, I am tempted to believe that there is something strange with that river.

11

GEORGE AND THE HYENA

Gomendi Maningi

I was a well-known and established drinker who cared not much for my safety or for my father's, more than the beer can that was in my hand. Childless, living half an hour away from other people, and a risk taker; all of these summed up who I was at the time. I lived with my father who was in his mid-70s and I was half his age. Since we lived away from other people, I loved going to the village that was nearby to socialize and kill time on Fridays and any day of the week that I felt lonely.

In that particular village, Kavimba by name, there were many kinds of beers. Homemade brews and canned beverages that were sold at the bar that was built on a high land. Whenever the radio of the bar was playing it could be heard more than five kilometers away, probably due to the plains that were on the north and western side of it. Between Kavimba, where the bar and my social life was to be found, there was a large animal corridor from the forest to the river.

Stubborn as I was, I refused to heed people's advices that I should spend the night in the village with them that night after we had drank a lot of beer. I insisted in returning home. In my pockets there two cans of beer and I held the other two in my hands. It must have been around 3am and the bar was operating all night. Leaving my friends behind, I vanished into the moonless night.

Something ran past me quickly when I was on the outskirts of the village. I could not figure out what it was because it ran quickly. I was now past the cemetery. I quickened my pace. It ran in front of me again. I sobered up quickly. If I did not become clever I was going to be eaten. Even if I screamed, nobody was going to come to my help for two reasons; I was far away from other people and could not be heard. If they heard me, no one would come for fear of the elephants, buffaloes and hyenas. Secondly, the only satellite police station in the area was many kilometers away.

My adrenalin levels went up. The hyena must have realized that I walked like a man who was not sane, for I was singing loudly and speaking with people that were not anywhere near me. I staggered from side to side in my walk. I threw at it with the beer cans that were in my hands, missing it. I was left with the ones in my pockets. I had by now managed to cover half the distance to where I was going. I whistled twice for my dogs that were at home. They came running and bucking, only their master called them by blowing a whistle twice.

The hyena ran and hid in front of me. I threw the other beers at it. The dogs reached me on time when I had nothing left to defend myself with. They chased the hyena away since their numbers favored them. All the beer I had drunk in the village got used up quickly. In the end I was humbled. Everything I had done that day was a waste. The money I used to get myself drunk and the one I used to buy the four unopened beer cans, were all wasted. Plus, I nearly got eaten by a hungry hyena.

I learned my lesson and the experience converted me. The only place I went to in the village during the next few days was church. My pride and bravery forsook me and I came back to my senses. Had I kept to the life I was living, I would not have gotten married. I may have been eaten by hyenas long ago, and that is not how I wanted to die.

12

SLEEP MY DOG

Elizabeth Goya

'There is no place I can run to my son. My husband and my three daughters have passed away. We long came to this place in the colonial times. It must have been twenty years since we left our home village and came here in search of a living. My husband found work herding cattle for the Colonial Development Corporation. Towards the late 50s we crossed over into Zimbabwe in search of greener pastures for ourselves. We settled at a place called Gwelo; a farming community. Sugar cane and milk were abundant in Gwelo. We had plenty of soap and life was good, but it was short lived. We were on the move again. I have gone to many places in my life. From Zimbabwe we moved to Zambia, by then Zimbabwe was Rhodesia and Zambia was North Rhodesia. We did not settle in Zambia. My husband found work at WENELA in Victoria Falls. They transferred him back to Botswana where he worked at a timber factory. With time we came back to this place, but by now he had taken another wife. We could not return to our place of origin, things had changed there.

My husband was given a piece of land to plow. We also acquired some livestock; donkeys and chicken. One night, a pride of lions came to our home and they slaughtered all the seven donkeys we had. For my family this was a tragedy. With them gone, we had nothing left to till our land with. I think the lions that came that night must have been around fourteen. The lionesses were teaching their cubs how to kill. We heard them from inside the hut and could do nothing. All the dogs hushed. At first they barked and made a lot of noise. One of my dogs was hit by a lion that night. It had wanted to be brave and defend the territory. What could I have done my son, those are wild beasts. In the morning when we woke up I went to fetch water at a stand pipe that is a distance away from my home. I returned from my errand at around 9am and found my dog striving to withhold its life from leaving it permanently. It must have been waiting for me to give it permission to die. I touched it gently and said 'sleep my dog, sleep.' Then it closed its eyes and breathed its last. It was a very precious dog to me. It could not die without waiting for me to bid it fare well. All the night it endured the pain until 9am.

Two nights ago a pride of four lions came again. It was two cubs and two lionesses. They passed a meter away from my hut walking towards the other hut. They ate all the puppies I had that were nested towards that area. I have no puppies right now. At times it is the hyena that comes around. I have nowhere to go. I will stay here until God tells me what to do. He is the one that knows why my husband and children all passed away living me in this lonely state. My husband loved his field and I cannot forsake it and move to another place. Yes, there are days when I have no food and I have grown old to walk to the water taps. I am grateful for the farmer's wife that often brings me water gallons twice a week and the other lady that brings me food every now and them.

My grandkids like it here but they do not live here. They come for a day and then they go. I do not blame you for delaying to help me, I blame the God that brought me on earth, but I will still trust him. He knows why I have to go through all of these. I believe I have a lot to teach people about love and peace. I have seen a lot in my life. The lions and hyenas come and go. I am used to being visited by them twice a week. I sleep at 5pm before the sun goes down because I have no one to talk to at night.

13
RUNNING NAKED

Highways A3 and A33 are unofficially known as the southern corridor into Africa, because of the long distance trucks that use them daily. The traffic that passes through A33 is mostly long distance trucks to and from Zambia, Democratic Republic of Congo, Namibia, Tanzania, Malawi, and South Africa. In the past the road has been badly damaged due to the heavy tonnage of the carriers, which in turn damaged the tires of some vehicles that used the road. Trucks are largely to blame for the damage, although they in turn are victimized by their own cause through tire bursts.

On one of the days a certain man drove his truck from Congo Libreville headed for South Africa. He had spent three days at the Kazungula border in Zambia waiting for clearance to cross the border into Botswana. The delay at the borders has also seen an increase in prostitution and an avenue for increasing the spread of the virus. One of the factors that lead to delay in crossing the border from either Zambia or Botswana is the use of ferry boats which at times are slowed down by a strong rush in the river current or faulty mechanics of the ferry boats. Having gone through all of these challenges he managed to cross the border, hoping to cross through Botswana in a single day so that he would load in Johannesburg and be headed up north within time.

Two hours into the country, being in between two towns, he experienced a tire burst on his double axel trailer. It was paramount that he replaces the tire for easier transportation of his cargo. Unfortunately for him he was travelling alone. He parked on the side of the road, careful not to go too much off the road into the soft sand, least he stuck. Fellow truck drivers stopped to help him. They struggled to remove and replace the tire. By now it was around 3pm and his plans to cross through the country had been disturbed by the delay.

The breakdown had also served as an opportunity for the men to socialize and get to know each other. By nature these men always help each other; they can never drive past a man in need for they know that it might be them one of the days. If he needs food or water they provide, since break downs vary in nature and can make some of them immobile for over a week. They managed to fix the tire then waited for him to set off first.

Before setting off he felt like going to the bushes for a bowel movement. He had enjoyed nshima with beef an hour ago in one of the towns he passed through. He unbuckled his belt and lowered his trousers and prepared himself to answer the call of nature. Unknown to him where he had stopped to attend to his tire there were three lions that had been resting on the trees nearby. They did not disturb the travelers in anyway all along. They did see that the men were not a threat to them thus they went back to sleep. Sensitive to every movement, they woke up as the intruder walked up to them, but they maintained their position. He did not know what he was walking into.

Perils of Tranquility

With his knees half bent and going down to stoop in the golden grass he shot up like a pressurized spring when he heard the charge of a lion that had been resting under the tree that he had chosen for the call of nature. In his shock at what might have become of him he left his pair of trousers behind, running towards his truck with no fabric of clothing on his body. Earlier while changing the tire he had removed his shirt. The men he had left behind were startled to see him running to his truck in that state. He was so scared he drove his truck with no clothing on. His friends knew what had happened way ahead when the fear was gone.

14

A KILL IN FRONT OF MY HOUSE

Dikeledi Merapelo

A civil servant visited our farm yesterday morning with his three colleagues. The madam of the house asked me to prepare tea for the visitors. I overheard one of the visitors asking her if it was possible for him to camp on our farm with his wife in future. He loved camping and they had all the camping equipment. She told him of what we had recently gone through.

Some days ago, our madam and the owner of the farm went quad biking with her husband in the evening. Her husband led the way and she followed him behind on her quad bike. Ginja, their dog, persistently followed her although she begged it to return home. 'Ginja, go home. Go back. Shoo shoo, go home.' The dog was hindering her ride and the gap between her and the husband increased. On their left were huge trees that made up the enclosed farm forest. On the right lay a vast open farm land of over fifteen thousand hectares. The sunflower had grown high and was six weeks from being harvested. The shadows of the trees were inclined south east. The songs of the birds reached mortal ears without any disturbance. It was really a good time for going out to enjoy the breeze that blew from the farms.

Perils of Tranquility

Rra Mphos turned his bike onto the main farm road from the turn off that went behind our house. Mma Mpho's bike came along behind him, with Ginja galloping behind her. She turned her head to chase the dog away as she had done before. Lo and behold there was no dog. Its tracks ended in the middle of the road and no further. Did a miracle happen! The dog had vanished.

The leopard that lives on one of the trees had snatched the dog away. It snatched the dog inches after she passed by. At the very moment the dog vanished, Mma Mpho had increased the speed of the quad bike. Had she maintained the same speed it is likely that it might have been her that could have been snatched by the leopard. The tranquility of the moment was very deceptive. The stubbornness of Ginja lead to his death.

We have cattle on the farm that attract predators. Our quarters are located not far from the cattle kraal. One early morning lions came to the farm. They scared the cattle causing them to run in panic in all directions. We heard from the noise outside that there was something wrong. One of the cows, realizing that it was soon to lose its life, ran in the direction of our quarters. The lions had no fear in giving chase towards our houses. They killed it in front of my house. It bellowed and groaned in pain. I profusely sweat though it was only 5am in winter. I had been pressed before the incident took place, but when the lions took camp in front of my house to eat their breakfast, I felt no need for going to the lavatory which is located outside the house. For an hour they ate the cow.

None of us went out of our houses during that hour least we added flavor to their meal.

They ended up leaving their meal as the sun rose. There was blood and dung all over the soil where they had killed the cow.

15
THE WATER BUCK

Gomendi Maningi

Some years ago George went herding cattle for the whole day in the plains of Matavanero. The drinking point for the cattle is at a place called Ndyambwene, a spot on the Chobe River. Across Ndyambwene is Sira, a settlement in Namibia. To the west of this spot is a pasture called Nansa, which is well known for the tall grass that grows in it. The first settlers of the Chobe Enclave gave various names to the pastures and parts of the river based on the history of the places. Ndyambwene means 'I got eaten with my eyes open'. The name is a result of the vicious crocodiles that live at that part of the river. They eat whatever man or animal that carelessly drinks water there.

It is a distance of many hours travelling by foot from home to Ndyambwene; the distance is much longer if one is driving animals along. Cattle move slowly while grazing. It is common that cattle herders reach the river at around 3pm and after the cattle have drunk they head back home with great speed so that the sun set finds them having reached home. For darkness to fall while someone is still in the plains, it means a sure death from whatever fierce animal that shows up.

On one of the days while George was at Ndyambwene with the cattle, his dogs startled a water buck that was hiding somewhere nearby in the grass. They gave chase with their master running behind them. A water buck is an antelope that is a shockingly poor runner. In no time the dogs had it surrounded. One of the dogs caught it by the hind leg; George hit it heavily on the head by the stick he was carrying. He hit it repeatedly until its lifeless body lay motionless on the grass. Since he was far from home and evening was approaching there was no way he was going to carry the whole antelope home with him. He sliced off its liver and lungs then hid the carcass in the tall grass so well that the hyenas could not detect that there was free meat lying nearby when they came to drink that night. He gave his dogs some meat to eat for the kill.

The select internal organs he brought home were evidence to us of fresh meat that lay out there. Though it has been over ten years since the incident took place, I still know how nice that liver tasted. Fortunately, there were only three people that were to enjoy the water buck at home. My cousin and grandfather did not like it; they called it donkey meat for it has much fur. They were being choosy, though they rarely ate an antelope in those days and the laws were too strict on killing wild animals. The trio of us enjoyed the liver. Before the sunrise the following day, George, I and our worker took off to get the rest of the meat. We took two empty sacks and some ropes. No dogs came with us. The reason for leaving home before sunrise was that no one would see us leaving and thus tell the authorities.

There is a dry river bed that has its source at the start of Iswiza plains next to our home and meanders all the way to Ndyambwene. We made a trail along the dry river. To the traveler who might have seen us at a distance, they might have thought that we were looking for a straying animal. I suppose this assumption was held by the soldiers who normally flew a white twin tailed plane daily around 9am across the plains on border patrols. It took us about two hours to get to the antelope. We cut the animal at the waist in two parts. I got to carry the hip and hind legs. Oh it was certainly heavy and I staggered all the way home. Though the load was that heavy I shouldered on all the way, dropping it to the ground only when we heard the sound of an approaching airplane. At the sound of it, all of us dropped and quickly covered the meat with dry grass then climbed up out of the river bed and pretended to have been looking for something. The stupid thing about the idea when I think of it now is that we forgot that the ground view from the sky is of a greater angle than what we assumed of it. In our minds we compared the ground view to an Ariel view; we assumed that the pilots were not to wonder at our sudden appearing into plain sight and looking in all directions without questioning our behavior. Such foolish thinking we had then.

We got home an hour to noon. The meat was too much for three people. Though we had overcome one problem of bringing the meat from Ndyambwene to our home, there lay another danger all together. With the water buck at home we had to devise a plan to make sure that the wildlife authorities did not detect it each morning when they came on patrols each morning. At that time of the year, hyenas were a nuisance each night and it was the duty of the game scouts to keep them away from us every night. Every morning they came to ask the same questions they asked all the time. By now we knew the routine. 'Good morning, did you hear any hyenas last night.' And our response was always the same. 'They were here last night after 10pm. We heard them calling from behind the kraal. One came from the east the other from the west.' That was the normal answer not because we had memorized but because it was what happened every night. Occasionally they would leave us after asking for a cup of fresh milk. Their visit was normally timed between 7:30am and 8am. We knew their schedule; we knew their movements like the shadows of the trees.

Since we were fully aware that the game scouts were definitely going to be coming every morning to our home, a plan had to be devised so that the meat remained hidden. They obviously knew the difference between beef and antelope meat just by looking at it and we were not going to risk being caught by letting the meat to dry at home by the time they showed up.

It became a habit that around 6am every morning we took the drying biltong to the forest to hang it up in the branches the whole day. With time we got tired of always running between home and the forest every morning and evening, and praying that we did not get caught and wishing at the same time that while the meat was drying up in the branches, no raven or scavenger would spot it and eat our hard earned meat. On the first day that the antelope died, we were over joyed and did not consider the possibility of things turning out the wrong way like they did.

Initially it was not our desire to always be running between home and forest twice a day avoiding being caught. We had hoped to enjoy the meat and unfortunately we never did. It was eaten hurriedly all the time. Everything that is done in a hurry is never enjoyed. In the end, the remaining meat was given away for free. I guess it is true that stolen fruits are sweet even if it is not for long.

16
THE PRICE OF ADULTERY

Silozungiro Civaka

There is a price to everything we do under the sun. A Congolese truck driver once gave a ride to a lady and her teenage child in Nata of Botswana. They were going to Kasane, three hours up north from where he picked them up. Both the driver and the woman were married people.

It is common for people who undertake long journeys to switch their minds to sleep mode once the tires of the vehicle start rolling. The son of the woman took off for dreamland immediately as the truck was going through the outskirts of the town. Seeing that the boy was fallen asleep he began to woo his mother, he did not want him to hear what they were going to be talking about, least he testify against his mother when he meets the father at home. I want to believe that their conversation went according to his expectations for somewhere along the way he parked the truck by the side of the road, the boy fast asleep still. He and the lady silently climbed out into the forest, leaving the engine running.

When the boy woke up he found the truck's engine idling with nobody around except himself. He waited for a while. Eventually he felt fear's grip squeeze his heart. All sorts of questions ran through his mind, with no answer to any of them. A twenty seven seater bus stopped to find out if there was anything wrong. He informed them he had been sleeping and did not know what happened to his mother and the man who drove the truck. The bus driver left the boy with the assurance that he was going to pass the message to the police who are based at Ngwasha Veterinary Gordon gate.

The police arrived and undertook a search in the forest that is along the highway. Not far from the truck they found remains of what used to be two people, a male and female. Their hands and feet were found there, other body parts were not found. On the scene on the ground were used male condoms. My assumption is that the man and woman at one point had had carnal knowledge hence the used condoms. I suppose there were lions that were resting in the place where they sneaked to relieve themselves of their sexual pressures, unbeknown to them of the danger they were walking into. They must have engaged in their inferiors deeds without any immediate fear of anything except of being caught by the sleeping boy. I suppose they were attacked and eaten after making love to each other. Probably the lions found them taking a break from their stolen moment of enjoyment, and gathering energy for one more pleasurable experience underneath those trees. They were strangers to each other who were going to be in each other's company for an average of only three hours, there after they would go their separate ways.

Both of them were wrong. None reached the destination. The pleasure of the moment catalyzed the nutritious processing of them in lions stomachs.

I do not lay the blame on the lions, rather I blame the two. If the man really wanted sex all the time what hindered him from changing jobs so that he could be with his wife daily, and what did he expect to gain by cheating on her. If she had a sexual problem with her husband what stopped her from seeing a counselor or talking out the problem with her husband. Infidelity is often paid for by a very high price by those that do not see any immediate danger in it.

17
A DAY AT THE GRAZING PASTURES

Luze Makonga

A couple of years ago when I was still a small boy it was my duty to herd my grandmother's cattle daily. At 8am every morning, I milked them and ensured grandmother had her tea with milk. If I delayed to bring the milk on time she got cross with me for it. Our home village is in Pandamatenga and our residence at the time was in an area of the village called Guest House, near the boundary line of Botswana and Zimbabwe.

One February morning, I drove the cattle to a grazing pasture known as Matshwane. Matshwane is a place where most of my relations had their plowing fields. We used it both for grazing and plowing crops. I was the only boy at home then, my other siblings lived in town. I think at that time our cattle were close to thirty nine, including seven calves. There are plenty of trees at Matshwane that provide shade to cattle herders all the time. Most of the time when we rest in their shade we are tempted to fall asleep; in our waking moment we find that the cattle have crossed the border line into Zimbabwe. None of us wanted our grandparents' livestock to cross into another country for the authorities on that side seized them and killed them to curb the spread of the Foot and Mouth Disease.

Towards noon of that day as I rested under the shade of a mopane tree, watching cattle graze at a distance, a small puppy like creature came to me. Honestly, I thought and believed it was a dog. I played with it for a while. It had lovely fur. Well, dogs have different breeds and I thought this was one of those dogs that are of a breed that I have not met before. It dashed off into the trees and it vanished out of sight in the same manner it came. Around 3pm it showed up again and we played some more. I did wonder though as to what a puppy, a beautiful rare breed puppy was doing all by itself far from home. I assumed it was lost. I had never seen the like of it at home before. Interestingly, we got along easily and this fascinated me. I liked the dog. About forty five minutes later it went away, this time it did not show up again quickly like it had earlier.

Towards evening I started driving the cattle home. I did not want darkness to fall with me still on the pastures for fear of lions and hyenas attacking the cattle. Towards setting of sun as I approached home I looked back and saw the puppy running far behind me coming. Surely I found myself a very handsome dog, and I thought to myself that I was going to be the only one in the village with that breed. I closed the cattle in the kraal and went into the hut to get maize flour to give to my grandmother who sat around the fire cooking. At the precise moment I touched the door handle of the hut, the handsome dog appeared.

'Granma, Granma, this is the dog I was just telling you about. See how handsome and strong it looks.' I said excitedly.

'Oh no, we are not going to get any peaceful sleep tonight. You have brought home a cub,' she said mournfully. She did not get to finish her statement before a roar of a lion tore apart the peace of the night. She crawled to the nearest hut. The lionesses had entered our compound. All the cattle in the kraal shifted to the front next to the gate, close to their owners. The dogs hid themselves behind the house. No dog was heard backing. The queens of the forest had come to collect one of them. I trembled that evening wondering what was going to happen next. My grandma did not own a gun. If she had one, we were going to shoot at them.

The roaring and charging of the lions took a long time. It was back in those days when we did not have any cellphones. Only those who had money afforded to own cellphones. The roar and charging of a lion is not as low as a dog's so it is audible even at great distances. None of our neighbors dared come to our aid. I think those who are most fearful had hid themselves under their beds that night.

The game scouts heard the commotion and came to our rescue. They managed to drive the raging lions away. The lions must have thought I stole the cub from them and that is why they were so mad. After they had gone there was no need for food. We did not feel the hunger in anymore, because we were so scared.

18

WAITING FOR DEATH

Ben‖oe

In our culture, when a man reaches the age that qualifies him for marriage, he has to drive a live antelope from the forest to the settlement where people reside. This is meant to prove that he is a man that can take care of his family. There are two antelopes that he has to drive home. The first he drives it on the day when his family asks for the lady's hand in marriage. When it reaches home he is the one that kills it and the meat is enjoyed by the community. He is then given the lady to go stay with until the day he thinks he is ready to marry her. On the wedding day, he does the same practice he did before to win the heart of her family. He drives another live antelope alone to the community in the evening; if by any chance he would have had kids with her before they get married he is required to drive two wild antelopes home. He is not allowed to kill the animal in the forest; therefore, he has to kill it with every villager looking on. That is the true mark of a man in our Ng‖oaca culture and throughout the entire khwedom world.

Xuri died at the age of 90 years. In his lifetime he saw great and wonderful days. There was a time he went hunting alone. He left early before dawn and headed south of our camp. He was tracking some antelopes. He went deep into the forest without coming across any animal. Back home his family needed some meat and he was the provider. The whole day he was away he did not kill anything. It was one of those bad days that even the experienced come home with empty hands. Lions and cheetahs experience the same thing once in a while, and they can take a couple of days without making a kill regardless of how much effort they put in.

About three hours past noon, he saw a lioness coming towards him from under the trees. On his sides were two other lionesses equally fierce like the one approaching him from the front. Death was certain if he acted foolish and slowly. Yes, there were those times when my tribe's people could chase away lions from the animals they had killed so that we got the meat in the end. But this was different. If he lingered a moment longer surely he was going to be dinner to the lionesses'. He took off at a great speed for home as though he was not in his late 70s by then. Home was five hours running distance from where he was. He had only two options; either give up and accept to be a late afternoon meal or force his aged legs to serve him one more time and hope his chest responded accordingly. Five hours running for life is not that easy, especially with three lionesses coming behind at full speed.

With time, the gap between Xuri and the beasts shortened. They closed in on him and he kept pushing his body forward. He gave the chase his best shot. The smoke rising above the trees from the camp appeared. His safety was within reach. At last he got in the camp and fell down from fatigue. Everybody gathered around him to know what was wrong. Unfortunately he fainted;

we did not know what had happened out there but we guessed he was running away from lions; that were the only probable reason as to why he came running at such speed and fainting. He became a hero in our community. Apart from him I know of no aged man who outran three lionesses for five hours consecutively. He has been the talk of the community since the incident took place.

In the end Xuri got tired of death. One early morning he rose up and filled a five liters bottle with water then went to the graves to await death to finally take him out of this life. The old man had had enough of the miseries of life here that he saw the only way out was not to run away from death anymore but to follow it. This may sound funny that the old man who at one point in the past did beat all impossibilities and ran faster than a pride of lions in his old age, was now sitting at the cemetery waiting for death to show up its ugly face from under the ground and take him to the place we all fear to go. He sat by an unmarked grave till the sun had gone high in the sky, occasionally quenching his thirst with the water. He waited for the most feared experience in a unique way and at the very place where we all finally end up at. Death did not come at a time when he expected it. If he had allowed it to take him away the day lions chased him he could have died, but not now. Who are we to summon it to our presence when we want? It comes at its own appointed time, especially when we are not ready. Xuri died years later from old age. His children took him home from the cemetery before noon of that day when he had gone to wait for death. He waited for it like a man waiting for a train coming from a faraway place.

19

A MOMENT AWAY

I spent the past weekend in the Namibian town of Katima Mulilo that is in the Caprivi region. After paying for a weekend accommodation at Mukusi Cabins, I took my KJV bible and went to church that very evening. I found church was over, people had gone home, and I was very late. I paid a visit to some relations that I had not seen in two years before going back to spend the night. Since I was so tired, I did not stay awake late into the night. I took a cold bath and then went to sleep.

A very loud crash woke me up in the early hours of the morning. Checking the time on my cellphone, it showed that it was after 2am. The crash sounded like that of a car having driven into one of the adjacent cabins. For fear of the unknown I did not want to get out of the room. I knew there was something wrong outside. Next I heard loud voices from the security guards knocking on a couple of doors calling out to someone to wake up and come to rescue the situation. My guess was they were calling out to the owners of the vehicles that had parked in front of the reception. By now I was confused, I had no idea of what was happening, but there was no doubt something was not right. The person they were calling out to, refused to wake up. Grabbing my clothes quickly and putting them on, I stepped out to see what was happening. I greeted them though they seemed to be in a hurry. From their talk I could tell there was somebody drunk somewhere in the whole picture. Fortunately the cabins were ok.

Less than a hundred meters from my room I figured out that the commotion came from the filling station that is beside the lodge. Cautiously walking to the scene I said a desperate silent pray, 'God help us. Burning to ashes isn't how I intend to die. I know it is not for me to choose, but not this way.'

As I approached the scene I saw that a couple of long distance truck drivers were already awake from their trucks and they were standing a few meters from the scene. A metallic maroon van had knocked over a fuel point on the filling station. There was a lot of petrol on the pavement. Pipes that pump fuel from underground tanks were exposed. The van had collided head on with a late 1980s Toyota corolla model on the main road that is about fifty meters from where it was now. Then it veered off to its right after colliding with the other car, to the Engine filling station where it not only knocked over the fuel point, but hit the metal pillar that supported the roof of the filling station head on. The post remained unshaken, but the van was the one that badly got damaged with the radiator and its engine forced back inwards. From my own analysis I think the van was not repairable. There was no one in the van when I got there. Somebody had been quick enough to rush the driver and the passenger to the hospital.

I circled around the scene taking photos for memory's sake. Another car pulled in a few minutes after. There was a bunch of drunkards inside it, smoking and drinking

Perils of Tranquility

beer. One of them walked towards the scene with a lit cigarette in his hand. He posed for a photo in front of the van, unmindful of the environment, and the petrol that was all over the pavement and the exposed fuel pipes from under the ground. I got furious at him for being such an imbecile for bringing a trigger to a massive explosion. Someone called out to him, angrily telling him to move away. Had he attempted to put off the cigarette, his natural reaction would have been to throw it down and stump it with his feet. This was going to be the most terrible thing to do under the circumstance. Somehow I cannot tell how the red ashes that fell from his cigarette failed to cause the petrol to explode. It was a miracle. There were two filling stations on the same area. One was exclusively for small cars, the other was for trucks. There were over five trucks that had parked for the night. Two buses that do business between Walvis Bay and this town were parked here for the night as well. Across the road is a Shell fuel filling station. Had there been an explosion, all three filling stations were going to simultaneously explode. All the guests that were sleeping in the lodge might have burnt to ashes in their sleep. Since it was Friday, I suppose that many of them had gone to bed having taken a lot of beer. I went back to my room and prayed that no other inconsiderate drunkard showed up that night with a lit cigarette in his hand to pose for a photo with a friend's cellphone camera or inspect the scene.

With what was happening outside, it took me longer to fall asleep. Finally, I fell asleep. In the morning when I woke up, the van was nowhere to be seen. They towed it away during the night. The nightmare of the weekend was far from being over.

The next day I was to leave the country for mine. I left the town in the afternoon at 3pm for the border. There is a fifteen minutes walking distance between the Namibian border post and the Botswana border post at Ngoma. There is a very wide river between the two countries known as the Chobe. Botswana is on the South and Namibia on the north at this point. The Botswana border is on a steep plateau and the Namibia one is at a lower altitude. Climbing the plateau into the country is really tiring. The hitching post is a kilometer further beyond the border post on the Botswana side at a gate for vehicles on transit through the Chobe National Park.

I stamped my passport upon entry and walked up to the hitching post as it was the only place that had reliable transport. Most of the vehicles from the border rarely give rides to hitch hikers.

There is a steep valley on the west up the plateau from the border. On the east is a forest that serves as a corridor for animals to the river. They rarely use the valley for its steepness and it easily makes them prone to predators. In the past, I heard stories of people that met with elephants on this short stretch of a road. A friend of mine once shared his experience when he drove through it in an open van. He told me he drove past an elephant as he descended to the border to drop off someone there. On his way back he met the raging elephant that he drove past earlier. He thought of driving swiftly past it. His analysis of its behavior and reaction were flawed. The

Perils of Tranquility

elephant got into the middle of the road as he neared it. He stepped on the brakes quickly and skidded. In an angry manner it extended its trunk to snatch out of the car any of the persons that were sitting in the open at the back. Remember that on the right is a steep valley, on the east is where the elephant was. There is a big cement cap that has been built between the lanes so that one cannot drive into the opposite lane. My friends told me it was a scary situation.

This was going to be my day as well. I have a tendency of making an 180 scan of the area when I am on it. I saw something moving under the trees at a distance right ahead. I stopped in my tracks to be sure of what it was. It was a large male elephant facing me flapping its ears. I determined not to put my step forward further than the other. To keep walking ahead would definitely be to risk a lot of things, including life itself. The elephant stood between me and the hitching post. There are normally armed soldiers and game scouts and the gate where I had to go. I saw no use of going back to the border for safety other than standing on the spot where I was. I moved my body and aligned it with a tall metal street light pole that is in the middle of the road. This I did with the assumption that the elephant would suppose that I was a part of the street light. I was not scared at all, was simply taking precautionary measures. I was too tired to run.

The Namibian car that I left at the border coming my way was already full that is why I had not got a ride in it earlier. The lady driving it found me standing me by the light pole in the middle of the road with my eyes fixed at a distance ahead of me. She figured out it meant an elephant or a buffalo. Thank God she gave me a ride to the hitching post where I got a ride in another car since hers was already full of people. I know some people say there was no danger in walking past the elephant. I was walking in the wild and not in the zoo. Theories and ideas have killed many souls in the past because they thought there was no danger in walking past a buffalo or an elephant. My will was not yet drafted. Let me go draft my will and sign it, and then I will come walk past the elephant or the buffalo. In the meantime, I dare not take the risk.

20
THE MAKING OF ULTIMATE RANGERS

Last year my uncle and I got a filming permit from the government for the making of a wildlife documentary titled Ultimate Rangers. There are two extremely dangerous situations we found ourselves in. The first was on a cold Sunday night. We got into the national park in the afternoon and spent the remaining part of the day filming. The permit afforded us a special privilege of going off road and staying by the animal we wanted to capture in film as long as we desired. Sunset of that Sunday found us at a place called Serondela inside the park. There was a lion and lioness that was the object of tourists' attraction. As everyone filled out of the park we remained behind for we could stay overnight until we had the footage we wanted.

We tracked the lions for eight hours that night. From 6pm to 2am. The male lion was not that old; it was the head of a pride of ten and was about 3.5years old. At sunset, the other 8 members of the pride were cuddling together 8km away by the river bank away from the two lions that had separated themselves to court. While away, the dominant lion in the pride fought with an older lion that was intruding in his territory. The intruder was captured days earlier by the game scouts in the eastern part of the district for it was eating farmer's cattle in Pandamatenga. It had gotten into the country from the Matetsi Hunting Area in Zimbabwe. Lions from

Zimbabwe have mastered a habit of getting in Botswana to kill cattle then go back to Zimbabwe where they are safe from being killed. Some come from Kazuma Game Park into Botswana then go back again for safety.

The fight between the two male lions must have been vicious for the dominant lion was wounded on the leg and blood oozed from it. We left the pair and went to film the eight that were sleeping away at the river. Taking longer at a scene helped us to capture the best moments. We were in no hurry. We spent time with our gaze on the sleeping lions, striving to keep our eyes from falling asleep. At 10pm there was some movement, they began waking up and we expected a serious action that night. We hoped for a kill if all lions were to wake up and start moving into the forest. Unfortunately we were wrong. They just changed places they were sleeping at. The movement was a sign that the pair we had left at Serondela was approaching, we could tell by the bigger lionesses' alertness. Cubs got back to enjoying the warmth of sleeping on top of one another. The pair arrived and the pride stood up to show respect to the dominant lion. There is order in the lion family than that of a common human family. When the head of the pride shows up, all rise to greet the dominant lion.

They then settled down again for about an hour. None did sleep; they were getting ready to go out hunting for impalas that normally graze around the abandoned airstrip. There was not much to capture on camera at this time. We switched the spot light off and the camera to relax since there was not much activity. The pleasure of spending so much time alongside the big cats is a rare experience of a lifetime. Somehow, I tended to get so used to being next to them that occasionally I had to remind myself that they were wild lions and not toys. I have realized that most people who lose their lives while filming in the wild do so as a result of losing touch with reality, and getting so used to being around dangerous animals that they start treating them as common. That is how we began feeling at this hour. The lions were not a threat to us; they were so peaceful as if we were not there. Such a feeling is really deceptive and should not be entertained.

During this moment of lack of alertness we were startled by the dominant lion springing up quickly into the air at lightning speed, I failed to capture in on camera. It jumped higher than the van we were in. The intruder had come to disturb the peace. A loud growl followed; all along we thought they were sleeping. The pride scattered in all directions, with the two big lions fighting each other for dominancy over the territory. This was the beginning of a long night. My heart pounded louder and the pulse increased. Neither I nor my uncle expected such a scenario; it was our first time encountering it. Before starting the engine of the car to follow them, the big intruding lion had already positioned itself towards the east of the safari car. The look on its behavior all suggested danger. None needed to tell the other that it was likely going to jump into the car. The safest thing was to get moving and follow the other lions that it had scattered.

With the vehicle moving as it tried to keep a pace with the lions, the big camera shook making it impossible to get a good footage. A number of them were running south west before we lost track of them. We searched for them using the headlights and the spotlight under the thickets and the trees. We had no idea where they had disappeared to. We turned the vehicle 180 to face the direction we came from. It was of great advantage to park in the open spaces where we could hear any approaching footsteps in the grass than parking at a blind spot.

Our eyes started feeling heavy no matter how hard we tried to stay awake. Eventually I fell asleep. I think my uncle fell asleep too, except he was smarter than me. His breathing was really low and controllable. Mine was heavy and one could easily tell I was asleep. He woke me up and told me that my breathing was likely going to get us killed, for lions were going to mistake me for a dying animal. Oh, it was already late; they thought there was a dying animal. Switching on the spotlight we saw a lion standing in front of the vehicle. There were no windows to shelter us in case it charged. The cabin of the van was grinded out, so we were in the open. We changed location to avoid being surrounded by many lions. We moved the vehicle and parked it facing west by a large acacia tree that had branches touching the ground. At least if we parked by the acacia tree it was going to keep us safe from being surrounded. Since it was now past midnight, we fell asleep again. There were tents at the back of the car, but there was no way we could pitch them in such a situation. If we stayed with the lions that night, chances were really high of capturing great scenes on camera.

I was woken up from my slumber by a couple of approaching footsteps in the dry grass. Though I woke up I did not open my eyes. I assumed the role of a child who needed protection from someone stronger. 'Uncle the lions are here now. Uncle, uncle, can you hear them. They are coming to us.' I whispered to him. After all he was my uncle and he happened to be older than me, so he knew what to do, but I knew he was as scared as I was. We switched the spotlight on. A total of eight lions formed a semi-circle around us and a ninth was approaching. Two of them were by the body of the car. Never have I been afraid in my life than on this night. For seventeen years in my uncle's life as a professional guide he had never met anything like this. It was a first for both of us. There was no security. We avoided talking to each other with them being so close. They were now aware we were aware of their intentions. Slowly, they left and formed a single file deep into the forest where it was impossible for us to follow them. This was a blessing in disguise. We had been granted to live through a rare opportunity, one that many are dying to experience. Enough for the night, rather for the early hours of the morning, our eyes could not keep open anymore though our hearts were pounding heavily like a distant ancient drum. We drove far away from the scene and parked besides the road by a big tree. I did not get any sleep regardless of how much I tried. Images of lions fighting and running away from each other kept flashing on my mind. I could not take them away. The roars and them wanting to get in the car to snatch us were fixed in my closed eyes. That was the only thing I saw.

The following day we hired a boat and went filming for half day along the Chobe River. Scenes from the river were unique in their own way. Elephants swimming in a single line across the river into an island, hippos feeding on large grass; it was lovely. The splendor of the moment must have been so great because we forgot to be on the lookout of keeping out of hippo territories. The waves slowly drifted the boat towards three hippos that were a distance from us. While the boat was being carried away silently by the waves, our bodies were turned away from the hippos. We were engrossed with capturing elephants that were by the river bank, when one of us turned on time to see a hippo approaching us from the back. The boat's engine could not be brought to life. Its water pump was submerged in water; this was a result of over cruising earlier on. Water had gotten into the water pump compartment, because the nose of the boat had been raised too high up and the engine submerged deeper and brought much closer to the body of the boat. This made it easier for water to get in the compartment of the water pump.

The dry land was way too far from us. The Chobe River is a wide river. Jumping into the water was not going to be helpful. The weight of the water getting into the boat increased. It is either we were to be killed by the approaching hippo or we were going to sink and if we managed to swim out, hippos that were by the river bank were going to finish us up. So it was a race against time; either we sink or the hippo kills us. We were then faced with the challenge of removing water from the boat and there was no container to quickly drain it out. Earlier before coming into the boat, I bought a small bottle of mineral water, about 500ml to quench my thirst. I brought it with me into the boat and it became useful at a time of need. It was not making any observable change in draining the water. It was too small. I had cut it in half using a pocket knife, to scoop more water. The hippo was getting closer and the boat was going down. I recalled that Presley had brought a larger container that is designed to store cold water when one is travelling. I found it lying somewhere under the chairs of the boat. His container was a life saver, in no time the water was out. The speed with which we drained it out is unbelievable. People tend to do things they cannot do under normal circumstances except when death is closing in on them. Oh yes, the boat gained balance and the water pump began working. We were out before the hippo reached us. It had been a close call, but was worth it.

21

TEN O'CLOCK IS MY TIME

During the years that my father had a passion for hunting, he had made it a principle that by 10am he ceased to hunt. His friends knew that he adhered to his principle of 10am. On one of his hunting trips, he was accompanied by my grandfather, and another friend of theirs, Mr. Kaisara of Kachikau. They took off to hunt buffalos beyond Kachikau at 5am on a Friday. After they had driven for a long time in the forest without seeing anything, they stopped and heard buffaloes mooing. The sound came not far from where they were. A large kraal of buffalo was by a pool of water. The three men sat down on the golden grass with their legs spread while devising a plan.

'Who is going to shoot first?' my father asked. 'Dan, you shoot first.' 'No, I cannot shoot; when one of you shoots I will run after the animal. Let one of you two old men aim at them and fire.' Their guns were resting on the ground, with the nose of the barrels pointing upward while they negotiated on the one that was to shoot first. In the end they settled that Kaisara should shoot. He stood up and took aim, using a 375 rifle. He hit one of the buffalos, and the whole kraal took off in all directions. Dan ran after the buffalo that was shot. He kept on its trail of blood that was oozing to the ground. He ran as quickly as he could after it. He came to his senses while he ran, he remembered he had been warned not to run in the tracks of a wounded buffalo for it could turn and

Perils of Tranquility

face where it was coming from. He got out of its trail and ran on the side.

Unbeknown to him the buffalo made a U-turn and took a side trail as well. Dan felt moist on his right arm. He wondered where the moist was coming from because he was not expecting it. The sun had rose high in the sky and the mist had long evaporated. He looked at his arm to see what was wrong with his hand. There was blood on his shirt, though he did not remember getting wounded. It was not his blood. He slacked his pace. Rose his head and barely two meters away from him stood a wounded buffalo facing him. Had he not been quick to raise his eyes and look ahead of him he would have ran into the buffalo. A wounded buffalo is more dangerous than a healthy buffalo.

The buffalo's eyes were closed, probably from pain and fatigue. He looked at his wrist watch. The time read 10:00am. He wanted to die knowing the time he died at, though it was not going to be of any use knowing the time. It was his time that he had set for himself to retire from hunting for the day. With speed he raised his gun. Acting with speed was essential if he wanted to live. Time was not on his side. He had to act quickly before the buffalo opened its eyes. The moment it opened its eyes, he was not going to survive. He sent a bullet through its head and it fell down right in front of him.

Kaisara and Masene heard the gun shot. But the sound came from far. The car could not reach the place. Dan took off his shirt and tied it on the shrubs to shield the dead animal from being seen by vultures. He ran back to the old men to come help him. None of the two hunters who were not present when the buffalo finally died believed that he shot it at such a close range. 'Dan where were you standing when you shot it?' one of them asked him. 'I was standing right where you are standing.' He answered them. 'You will get us in trouble. What were we going to tell Naluca your mother if you had been killed?' A dialogue between them began. Dan had acted to defend himself.

They took out their knives and skinned it. It was a fat buffalo. They hanged the meat on top of a tree and let it drip blood and dry while they all went home to get a donkey cart. Donkeys could easily maneuver the trees than a car.

On their way back on Monday, they heard a tree crack. 'Our tree has fallen' Dan said. 'No it is an elephant that is breaking down a branch from another tree,' one of the man said. Upon reaching the place they found out that it was their tree that had fallen off. The meat was too heavy to be held by the tree in their absence. There were tracks of hyenas on the ground. All the meat was eaten by hyenas; there was not even a single piece left.

Their hard earned meat was lost to scavengers. They killed a kudu to replace the buffalo. Their hunting permits allowed them to kill an antelope as well.

22
GATHERING FIRE WOOD

Last year July my aunt went to gather fire wood with a friend in the forest not far from the village. The forest south of Kavimba is made up of valleys and plateaus. Our home is built on a valley. The two women went in the forest in the late afternoon. They did not go far; they went to the back of the village. Some cattle were grazing on the area where they chose to gather wood.

They gathered enough and set about to tie them into bundles. Two carnivorous animals the size of our big dog came running and cattle ran away. The other lady called for Constance to come to her side and tie her bundle there. Constance refused to go. Her friend insisted, but she kept refusing. The dog looking like creatures had ran past between the ladies. They drove the cattle back again in the opposite direction. Some of the cattle raised their tails up and took off at high speed. The raised tails signaled to the ladies that something was wrong. They abandoned their wood and ran home. None of them had expected danger from so close to home.

The following day they heard that two adult lionesses had killed a cow somewhere on the north east of where they were gathering firewood. They figured out that what they had previously called dogs were actually cubs that were trying to drive the cattle back to their mothers so that the lionesses could kill more of them. None of the ladies had paid close attention to the dogs that were chasing the cattle. Later that day they went back to get their wood. They were very cautious, not wanting to be seen by lions of the previous day, just in case the lions were still close.

23
PLEASE HELP ME

Many years ago before Kavimba village was populated there were some people who lived in it who were not from the northern part of the country. A certain lady who was married to a man called Nfiyauzi, went to the river one morning with a group of other ladies to watch hippos. None of the ladies in the group knew anything about hippo behavior. This might have been due to their background and how they were brought up. All of them came from south of the country where there were no large rivers and no hippos.

When they reached the river bank they stood there watching a swimming hippo. In their ignorance they made a lot of noise while they stood on the river bank. The excitement must have made them to think there is no difference between a hippo and a domesticated goat. The ladies stood on the banks of Itenge river which serves as a boundary line in the Chobe Enclave between Botswana and the country of Namibia.

Without any warning, the hippo came charging out of the water. The ladies ran in panic back home. Unfortunately most people who are in their middle ages cannot run as fast as they did when they were still young. Nfiyauzi's wife was out ran by her fellows. She was caught by the raging hippo which tore her apart with its mouth, cutting her in two pieces. The upper body and the lower body were cut in two at the waist. A hippo has a very cruel way of killing people; this is how they generally kill their victims.

She was attacked close to the river bank for she fell with her upper body on the shallow waters. Her mournful call for help was heard even at long distances. 'Help me, the hippo is killing me.' When her upper body was raised up, so that the head maintained its normal position like when one is seated down, and the upper part of the waist made to touch the ground, she could speak though she was dying. Only a few people came to her help for fear of the hippo. Her life was ended in a very touching manner.

The Vekuhane people who live along the river are well acquainted with hippo behavior and they rarely get killed by them. For many years since the incidence took place nobody has been killed by a hippo, instead hippos continue to be killed in Mavere village if they are found eating crops in farms. They are killed for being pests, and some of the villagers eat the hippos. It's a very interesting way of life. as long as they do not lay a foot in the farms they are safe.

24

THE PREGNANT TEENAGER

Last week Wednesday night in Pandamatenga village a lion came late in the night and ended up killing a donkey that was in a kraal. Neo, a girl in her late teens who is expecting, was sleeping in her house. That night she was the oldest at home. Her mother had gone to sleep in a faraway home like she often does on every night. Neo slept in the house with her siblings. She was woken up by their dog running all over their compound.

Her head was resting on top of her arm, and the head was facing the entrance of the house. She opened her eyes and saw a lion chasing the dog around. She did not wake any of her siblings, for fear the children would scream out loud and the lion come for them. The moon shone brightly outside and it was easy to see what was happening.

She prayed to God to keep the dog from running into the house. Our dogs run to their masters when they feel helpless, especially when being chased by a lion. Her physical state was not going to allow her to run to safety if they were attacked. It seemed the lion wanted to eat the dog, but the dog kept running all over the place. The lion must have been very hungry, for it to settle upon eating a dog. Eventually it gave up on chasing the dog and went to the neighbors where there were donkeys in a kraal. The donkey kraal has been made of barbed wire.

Boitshoko Jeremia

I have no idea how the lion managed to go through the barbed wire and kill the donkey. Some years ago a lion had failed to get into that kraal. It was hindered by the kraal, but last week Wednesday night it managed. The neighbors did not hear the donkey being killed. In the morning they found its remains.

25
DIE HARD WARTHOGS

Kasane is a well-known tourist destination in southern Africa. Apart from being famous for the elephants that live in the Chobe district, it is also well known for the many warthogs that roam the streets and the baboons that often eat from trash cans in residential areas when people have gone to work. The baboons are a nuisance, up town in Plateau and in another location called White City they are really mean. I know of homes where baboons got inside kitchens when they found the windows or doors open, and they spilt everything on the ground. In one home there were small children that were left at home alone and they were afraid of the baboons so they let them have their way.

Matengu drives a taxi in the resort town of Kasane. At least once a month or once in two months I get a ride with him. Last week Friday I was in his taxi and we happened to talk about the warthogs of Kasane that have got so used to living around people like goats. Matengu told me there was a day he was driving from church in the evening. His church is not far from the river front. He turned left into the main road that is on down town Kasane. As he approached the Water Affairs offices a warthog got in the road from the left side. He veered off to the right to avoid running into it. The warthog did not stop nor did it retreat. It never goes back, it always goes forward. It went into the road and he hit it really hard. He stopped, his car had got damaged from the collision and strangely the warthog rose up, raised its tail and took off as if it was not terribly knocked over by his taxi.

He took his taxi that evening to a mechanic called Tom who also operates a taxi. Tom seemed not surprised at what Matengu had been through. A few days before Matengu ran into the warthog, Tom also ran into a warthog by an SUV in down town Kasane. He drove over it with the two front wheels and the vehicle got slightly raised from having the warthog under it. He reversed to take it out. He thought it was dead. To his shock it was not dead. It rose up and ran away.

Up until Matengu told me the story I had no idea warthogs are made of steal. The creatures do not die easily. Matengu could not believe it too, neither did Tom.

26
MATAVANERO

If it is your first time hearing the name Matavanero you would think it is a Madagascan town, it sounds more close to Antananarivo. If that is what you thought, you were deceived. It is found in northern Botswana; on average it has a population of three people annually. Of all places on earth I feel more at home in Matavanero than anywhere else. It was once inhabited by many people in the past then they began moving away to Kavimba to be close to basic facilities such as the clinic, cleaner water, and the primary school. Most of the families that moved away left their cattle behind for there were already many cattle where they were going, and taking cattle along meant overstocking grazing pastures. So they left them behind and opted to be coming every morning to Matavanero to check on them, and then go back in the evening to Kavimba.

A number of those who had left their cattle behind employed men to look after their livestock all the time. These herd men after sometime would get tired of staying far from people and in the end they quit their jobs. Before they quit their jobs, if they drank beer they spent nights in Kavimba or Seriva where did not feel lonely. Often than not the owners of the cattle had to go back to Matavanero and spend the nights because there was no one staying with them.

On my first year at University my cousin Othusitse and I had to go to Matavanero to the cattle. There was always much work to do. There was a day he and I dug a well to be watering goats from. It was too much work. There are many things I did with Othusitse, although he is one of those few cousins that can let you get killed by wild animals and run away. There was a morning we drove our cattle into the forest, and we had something walking in our direction. We looked under the trees and saw six buffalos walking towards us. He and I looked at each other; in our midst was our herd man. I turned my head to look back at the buffalo. Then I turned back to Othusitse and Bashi to figure out what was going to be our plan of escape. To my surprise Othusitse had already taken off running. He had created a very wide gap between us that was not easy to close. We finally caught up with him out of the forest. 'Why did you take off like that without telling us?' I asked him. I still remember his response up to this day. 'One of us has to live and tell the story of what happened. If we die who will tell those who are at home what happened! That is why I did not want to tell you. If I told you we were all going to be killed.' The truth of the matter is that he was afraid we could outrun him that is why he did not tell us. He knew if he told us he was going to be left behind, so he decided to take off first. From that day I knew that I had to be on alert all the time in the forest with him. He always wanted to save himself first before others. I think almost everybody can do what he did.

In Matavanero jackals used to eat our goats and hyenas enjoyed eating our cattle. The hyenas were really bad; they ate the cows without killing them. Once in a while

Perils of Tranquility

a cow would arrive home with its udder ripped off or without a tail. They ate the cows while they moved.

Almost every evening in winter through August and September elephants passed by our home from the forest to the river and back into the forest again. The grumbling of their stomachs as they moved in the trees close to us made so much noise that if one did not know it was the grumbling of the stomachs, one would easily get scared and pack their bags the following morning and go back. From drinking water at the river one or two elephants had a habit of coming by our home to eat the green mulberry trees for all the trees in the forest would have shed their leaves. In the morning when waking up we got to see elephant tracks all over our place. In the night when they walked past the house we never heard them. They walk silently.

Waking up in the night to go and pee was often a challenging experience. Inside the hut there is no toilet, the forest is the toilet. Since it is a no go area at night, we made a place at the back of the reed compound just for peeing only, and not for bowel movements. Even getting out of the house to go at the back of the reed compound, meant we walked carefully on the lookout just in case there was an elephant nearby. It was scary sometimes. Where there was moonlight it was often better. I remember a night in which elephants made a lot of noise and some of them were fighting not far from home. The short gun that we owned was not power full enough to kill an elephant. Our neighbor is the one who owned a powerful gun. That night some elephants came to his house and wanted to drink water from his water tank. He shot one of them in the stomach and it went back into the forest, I do not think that the elephant lived for long with that wound. I was really afraid that night I got and dressed and set on my bed. I admit I was so scared. I dressed up just in case they became really wild. The following day I was ok, all fear was gone. This was the place I grew up and there never was a day in which elephants came and attacked us in our houses, except for a single incidence that happened many years ago in Kachikau in which seven elephants walked into Liswani Secondary School and did not find their way out. Prior to that they had been to a certain home where they scared off some children. It was very dark that night. One of the elephants stood by the entrance of the hut. It was also raining. The boy wanted to move from one hut to the other. He did not know that an elephant stood at the door. He got out and walked between the front legs unaware that he was underneath it. After his eyes had adjusted to the darkness he could tell that he was in the middle of four strange pillars that he did not know off. He did not go further. He went back into the hut. There were many elephants in that compound that night. Since that day we have not had a similar experience anywhere in Chobe.